COCONUT OIL

65 RECIPES FOR COOKING CLEAN

COCONUT OIL

65 RECIPES FOR COOKING CLEAN

WRITTEN & PHOTOGRAPHED BY

RITIKA GANN

FRONT TABLE BOOKS | AN IMPRINT OF CEDAR FORT, INC. | SPRINGVILLE, UTAH

ISBN 13: 978-1-4621-2082-6

Published by Front Table Books, an imprint of Cedar Fort, Inc.
2373 W. 700 S., Springville, UT 84663
Distributed by Cedar Fort, Inc., www.cedarfort.com

Library of Congress Cataloging-in-Publication Data on file.

Cover and page design by M. Shaun McMurdie

Edited by Nicole Terry and Jessica Romrell

Printed in the United States of America

10 9 8 7 6 5 4 3 2 1

Printed on acid-free paper

SCAN to visit

www.randmcooks.com

For the loves of my life, my family.

CONTENTS

ACKNOWLEDGMENTS

This cookbook was dreamed up with the full support of my incredible and loving family to whom I dedicate this, my first official publication. First, to my mother and father—my pillars in life—I can't thank you enough for your unwavering support of my "unconventional" dream. Both of you were always ready to lend a helping hand in the conceptualization and practical aspects of my cookbook. Following this dream was only possible because of your support. To my sister, Mimi, I credit my ability to imagine and dream beyond the limits of "the usual." You are always full of new and exciting ideas and always ready to share your creative mind. Finally, I thank my husband, Michael, who, with such intensity and care, poured his time and effort into this book just as if it were his own. My dear family, without you, my dream would still be just a dream.

I would like to especially thank my mother again for giving me her time. Many an hour was spent helping with photography, lighting, cleaning, and a million other things. Mamma, you were my biggest inspiration and my greatest ally throughout this journey.

My very deepest thanks to my incredible sponsor, Maison Orphée, a company that is (like me), proudly Canadian, and the producers of the highest quality coconut oil that I have ever had the pleasure of cooking with. Thank you for seeing potential in this cookbook, and in me.

To my talented editors, marketing gurus and designers at Cedar Fort Publishing and Media—I can't begin to thank you enough for taking a chance on a young and passionate food lover. Thank you for incorporating my vision into this book, answering a million questions, and giving me honest feedback and meticulous instruction for my first experience in publishing.

And finally, I thank the hundreds of entrepreneurs, artists, and visionaries who have galvanized me: thank you for your art, advice, and strength.

COCONUT OIL 101: THE LESS-IS-MORE METHOD OF COOKING

There'll be no sweeping statements here; I won't promise that coconut oil is the magic key to losing weight, or that it'll cure cancer or the common cold. I'd like to differentiate between coconut oil, butter, and all the other oils that people love to cook with and explain my reasoning for using coconut oil for all of my culinary creations—with facts.

EVERYTHING IN MODERATION

First, let's address the confusion from conflicting reports (coconut oil is *the best oil* vs. coconut oil will slowly kill you). I like to think about it simply, oil is oil, and we need it to cook and bake—so it's unrealistic to assume we can eliminate something that essential from our diets. However, it's a matter of how much you use that is directly related to whether something is healthy or not. Deep frying something in a vat of oil is going to be unhealthy no matter what kind of oil you use—coconut, canola, or any other. That being said, if we really want to break it down and understand exactly what is in the oils that we're using, this chapter will give you a good idea of the types of fats in the oils we use every day.

FATS IN OILS

All the oils we're talking about are made up of saturated, monounsaturated, and polyunsaturated fatty acids. I'll be upfront: coconut oil does contain high levels of saturated fat.

However, while monounsaturated and polyunsaturated fatty acids are nutritionally desirable in cooking oils, the saturated fat content in coconut oil causes the oil to take a denser shape. Having a denser quality, the chemical composition of coconut oil holds a higher cooking temperature. In short, it takes far less coconut oil to shallow fry, bake, and sauté.

For example, where I would use 2 tablespoons of canola oil or olive oil, I only have to use 1 tablespoon—sometimes even less—of coconut oil to achieve the same level of browning, or moistness, or crispness.

2 tablespoons of canola oil = 248 calories

2 tablespoons of olive oil = 238 calories

1 tablespoon of coconut oil = 17 calories

If we're looking at calories, coconut oil will win by a landslide. If you're still concerned about the saturated fats, remember that many physicians have responded to the allegations against coconut oil and astutely pointed out that if you're maintaining a healthy and balanced diet, one ingredient alone will not cause heart disease or a raised cholesterol level; your diet must be approached as a whole if you have, or fear having, cholesterol or heart issues.

In fact, the AHA (American Heart Association) recommends about 13 grams of saturated fats in your diet (a little more than a regular tablespoon) per day.[1] In keeping with the theme of less is more, you'll notice that the vast majority of the recipes in this book comply with exactly this recommendation. How can this be? As was mentioned before, a little goes a long, long way with coconut oil. Cooking a feast for four can easily contain the appropriate amount of coconut oil in compliance with recommended intakes. For a healthy, active individual, coconut oil in these low quantities is right on par with the AHA's advice!

MORE BENEFITS OF COOKING WITH COCONUT OIL

Are you lactose intolerant? Many of us are! Butter sometimes causes unpleasant indigestion. Coconut oil is a fabulous alternative for those of us who can't digest butter easily.

There are also an increasing number of people who have chosen to adapt their diets to accommodate vegan eating. This means no butter. However, coconut oil can be used to achieve a very similar result in baking.

Another benefit? The flavor! Although not everyone appreciates the flavor of coconut, in all these recipes, coconut oil is an exceptional addition and brings out a beautiful flavor to the food that you can't get with any other oil.

ASIDE FROM COOKING...

I'd like to point out that coconut oil is not only for cooking, but is also beneficial as a topical treatment for dry skin, acne, brittle hair, and cracking heels. Talk about an all purpose ingredient! If it's in your pantry, you can use it for more than just cooking.

TYPES OF COCONUT OIL TO USE

In the creation of this cookbook, I exclusively used Maison Orphée's Raw Virgin Coconut Oil, a high quality oil with an ideal consistency. When you're looking for coconut oil to cook with, make sure you leave "cold-pressed" and refined coconut oil on the shelf. The healthiest and most natural coconut oil is Raw, unpressed, virgin coconut oil—although it does have a potent taste and smell.

The bottom line? Coconut oil can be used in global cuisine without compromising the integrity or flavors of traditional food; the sixty-five recipes that this book contains are intended to use little oil, and whole, unprocessed ingredients. You can continue to enjoy varied and colorful lunches, dinners, and snacks every day.

If you're still unconvinced, don't worry, all these recipes can be cooked with other oils as well.

---

1. https://healthyforgood.heart.org/Eat-smart/Articles/Saturated-Fats

AUTHOR'S NOTE

Before making any dietary changes, it's important to consult your family physician. The content in this chapter is strictly informational and based on studies, reports, and nutritional journals, but should not be construed in any way as an official medical recommendation.

SAUCES, SALSAS, AND CHUTNEYS

CHILEAN PEBRE

MAKES: ROUGHLY 1 CUP | TOTAL TIME: 10 MINUTES

Pebre is a spicy and flavorful Chilean salsa-condiment hybrid that has multiple variations. Pebre, in Chile is as ubiquitous as ketchup, and is commonly used as a spread for sandwiches and rolls in addition to being used as a condiment. There is no one traditional recipe–generations of Chilean families have combined their favorite flavors and passed down their own versions of the pebre recipe.

DIRECTIONS

1 Combine all the ingredients except the water in a medium sized jar. Add in the water and stir again. Let the ingredients soak for about 3 minutes.

2 If you want a less chunky pebre, pureé the ingredients in a food processor or blender.

Serve your pebre with chips or bread.

INGREDIENTS

8 scallions, finely diced

1 large tomato, finely chopped

¼ cup fresh cilantro, finely chopped

1 jalapeno pepper, de-seeded and diced

4 garlic cloves, minced

3 Tbsp. red wine vinegar

1 Tbsp. curly leaf parsley, finely chopped

1 Tbsp. chili sauce

juice of 1 lime

½ Tbsp. coconut oil

½ Tbsp. cayenne pepper

1 tsp. sea salt

2 Tbsp. water

CHIMICHURRI MARINADE

MAKES: 1 CUP | TOTAL TIME: 10 MINUTES

Both Uruguay and Argentina have laid claim to the invention of chimichurri sauce. The combination of cilantro, parsley, and the citrusy flavor is rumored to have first emerged as an invention of cowboys, who used it to flavor their meats as they roasted game on the open prairies. One particular origin story speculates that the name "chimichurri" was derived from the word "tximitxurri" which was brought over by the Basque settlers who came to Argentina. The word literally means "a rough mixture of things." Quite apt for chimichurri sauce that is a combination of so many herbs and flavors!

DIRECTIONS

1 Place all ingredients into a food processor and pulse until well blended. Let the sauce sit for 10 minutes before using.

Use this chimichurri sauce as a marinade for chicken, steak, or sausage. Marinate meat for at least 30 minutes soaked in the sauce before grilling or baking.

INGREDIENTS

¾ cup fresh cilantro

½ cup Italian flat-leaf parsley

6 shallots, finely diced

3 cloves of garlic, peeled

2 jalapeno peppers, de-seeded

juice of one lime

1 Tbsp. of red wine vinegar

1 Tbsp. coconut oil

½ tsp. cayenne pepper

¼ tsp sea salt

¼ tsp. black pepper

CLASSIC PINE NUT AND BASIL PESTO

MAKES: ½ CUP | TOTAL TIME: 10 MINUTES

Pesto has been around for centuries - the origin of pesto can be traced back to the early 16th century in Northern Italy; specifically, in Genoa. Although there are now variations (no doubt to address mounting concerns over nut allergies), classic pesto was historically made with fresh basil leaves and crushed pine nuts. Pesto can be baked into bread or served as a sauce, but traditionally, Italians are proud of serving it as a pasta sauce.

INGREDIENTS

- 2½ cups fresh basil leaves
- ¼ cup coconut oil
- ¼ cup fresh parmesan cheese, grated
- ¼ cup whole pine nuts
- 3 cloves of garlic
- juice of half a lemon
- 1 tsp. pepper
- ½ tsp. salt

DIRECTIONS

1. Blend together all the ingredients in a powerful blender or food processor. Pulse for 1 minute, then scrape down the edges of the food processor/ blender and pulse again until smooth.

Serve pesto with cooked pasta, or as a spread on whole wheat toast.

COCONUT AND RED CHILI CHUTNEY

SERVES: 4 | TOTAL TIME: 15 MINUTES

From the kitchens of South India, this delicious, savory chutney is a staple side that is served with many South Indian dishes. Chutneys are common in India and can be made out of most fruits, but the most popular of chutneys remains coconut chutney. They are seen more as relishes than sauces. In addition, colonization by the British spread the good taste around, and chutney is common in South Africa and in Caribbean countries as well.

DIRECTIONS

1. In a food processor, pulse coconut, ginger, chilies, and garlic, stopping to scrape down the sides of the food processor periodically. Add water a tablespoon at a time, after scraping down the food processor. Pulse until mixture comes together.
2. In a small frying pan, heat coconut oil, and add mustard seeds to the hot oil. Seeds will start to "pop." Turn off the heat after 1-2 minutes, and add in a sprig of curry leaves. Swirl the oil over the curry leaves.
3. Pour oil mixture over the coconut mixture and mix well, dispersing mustard seeds and oil evenly throughout before transferring to a serving bowl.

Serve chutney with idli, dosa, or utthapam.

INGREDIENTS

¾ cup freshly grated coconut

½-inch piece of ginger

5 red chilies, de-stemmed

2 cloves of garlic, chopped

3 Tbsp. water

1 Tbsp. coconut oil

½ tsp. mustard seeds

1 sprig of curry leaves

PIRI-PIRI MARINADE

MAKES: 2 CUP | TOTAL TIME: 15 MINUTES

This powerhouse sauce is full of flavor and used to spice up chicken. The popular restaurant chain "Nando's" put piri piri chicken on the map. It's commonly agreed upon that piri piri sauce sprung to life after Portuguese settlers arrived in Africa in the 15th century–specifically in Angola and Mozambique. This is where the star ingredient, African Bird Eye Chilies, were readily available. The name piri-piri means "pepper pepper" in Swahili.

DIRECTIONS

1. In boiling water, rehydrate red chilies for 5-10 minutes. Drain water and chop the stems off the chilies and add the chilies to a food processor.
2. Add the remainder of the ingredients to the food processor and pulse until thoroughly blended.
3. Pour mixture into a shallow saucepan and simmer while stirring for 8–10 minutes.

Use the piri piri marinade as a serving sauce with tortilla chips, or use as a spicy marinade for chicken or pork.

INGREDIENTS

⅓ cup dried red chilies (or African Bird Eye Chilies, if you can find them)

1 red onion

1 tomato, peeled and diced

2 red peppers, de-seeded and chopped

4 cloves of garlic, minced

¼ cup distilled white vinegar

zest of 1 lemon

juice of two lemons

2 Tbsp. coconut oil

1 Tbsp. white or brown sugar

1 Tbsp. crushed bay leaves

¾ Tbsp. fresh oregano, chopped

½ Tbsp. smoked paprika

½ tsp. sea salt

½ tsp. pepper

HOT SALSA VERDE

SERVES: 5 | TOTAL TIME: 20 MINUTES

Salsas in general can be attributed to the Ancient Aztec culture of Mexico. The process of combining the flavors of tomatoes, chilies, and other herbs is made even more flavorful with variations like salsa verde that uses tomatillos (green tomatoes), thus inspiring the name "salsa verde" which means "green salsa."

DIRECTIONS

1 Set your oven to broil. Slice each serrano pepper and remove the seeds. Place tomatillos, onions, and serrano peppers on a baking sheet. Brush them all with the coconut oil and broil for 10 minutes until the green tomatoes and onions are browned. Remove from the oven and let it cool down.

2 Once the vegetables are cooled, dice the green tomatoes, serrano peppers, and onions. Add garlic, cilantro, and ground pepper to a food processor. Pulse until completely blended.

Serve the salsa verde with corn chips.

INGREDIENTS

4 green tomatoes (tomatillos)

½ Spanish onion, cut into quarters

3 serrano peppers

1 Tbsp. coconut oil

1 garlic clove, minced

¼ cup of cilantro, chopped

1 tsp. pepper

SPICY PEANUT SATAY SAUCE

MAKES: 1 CUP | TOTAL TIME: 10 MINUTES

Peanut sauces are widely used both in Asian and African countries; especially Indonesian, Malaysian, and Vietnamese cuisines. The sauces are used as sides to seafood rolls and crispy wontons, or mixed in with noodles. Satay sauce can also be used as a marinade for skewers of meat. In Indonesia, peanut sauce is called "bumbu kacang," and is popularly eaten with gado-gado—a salad.

DIRECTIONS

1. In a small grinder or blender, pulse together all the ingredients until satay sauce is smooth and slightly runny.
2. Pour the sauce into a small pot and simmer, stirring intermittently for 5-6 minutes. Transfer to a separate bowl to serve.

Serve your satay sauce as a dipping sauce with spring rolls, or use as a marinade for chicken skewers.

INGREDIENTS

- 1 cup full fat coconut milk
- 4 Tbsp. smooth peanut butter
- 3 red chilies
- 1 Tbsp. honey
- 1 Tbsp. hoisin sauce
- 1 Tbsp. water
- ½ Tbsp. red curry paste
- ½ tsp. coconut oil

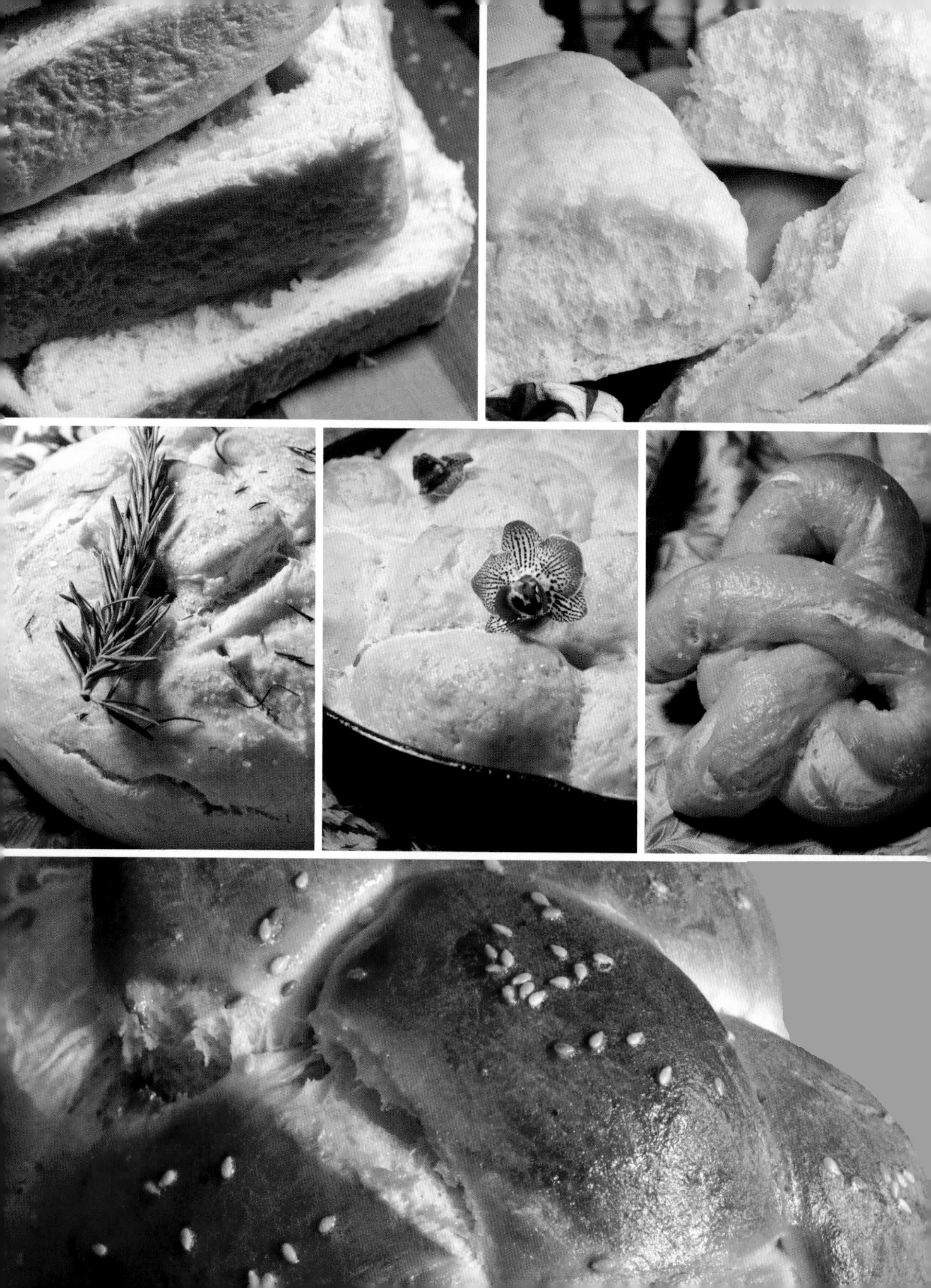

THE BREAD BOX

AMISH WHITE BREAD

MAKES: 1 LOAF | TOTAL TIME: 40 MINUTES

The Amish communities of America sure know how to make their daily bread. Amish white bread is a staple on their dinner tables. Bread making is regarded as a test of faith and patience, undoubtedly because of the time it takes to proof and rise, and the difficulties that can arise from bread making. The act of bread making is also closely tied to spirituality and scripture, as the bread made is often served at church communion.

DIRECTIONS

1 Grease a loaf tin with coconut oil and preheat your oven to 375 degrees. In a large bowl, whisk together warm water and warm milk. Dissolve brown sugar and instant yeast in the milk and water. Whisk thoroughly. Set aside for 10 minutes until mixture froths.

2 Whisk in coconut oil and salt. Sift in one cup of flour at a time. Knead until dough is smooth and elastic. Grease the sides of a large bowl with coconut oil and place the dough inside. Cover with a clean, dry towel, and let the dough rise for at least 1 hour (until doubled in size).

3 Punch the dough down and shape into a log. Place the dough into the prepared loaf tin. Let the dough rise for 40 minutes (it should fill the loaf pan and rise above the lip).

4 Bake for 30 minutes in the preheated oven.

Slice bread and store in an airtight container until ready to eat.

INGREDIENTS

½ cup of warm water

½ cup of warm milk

1 Tbsp. brown sugar, lightly packed

1 Tbsp. of instant yeast

2 Tbsp. coconut oil, plus extra for greasing

½ Tbsp. sea salt

3 cups of all purpose flour, sifted

HAWAIIAN SWEET ROLLS

MAKES: 12 ROLLS | TOTAL TIME: 2 HOURS

In the late 1950s, a bakery was born. Robert Taira, the founder, eventually found so much success that he relocated and changed the name of his bakery from Robert's Bakery, to King's Hawaiian. A typical bun that was found at the bakery was slightly sweet with a tangy flavor. The bakery became extremely popular, and the recipe for the King's Hawaiian bun was coveted. Now, national fast food chains market certain sandwiches made on King's Hawaiian buns.

DIRECTIONS

1 Preheat your oven to 350 degrees. In a large bowl, combine all the dry ingredients and the ginger together. Stir until well dispersed.

2 In a separate bowl, whisk together pineapple juice, coconut oil, coconut milk, honey, vanilla extract, eggs, and egg yolk. Whisk until completely smooth. Pour into the dry ingredients, combining slowly with a spatula. Dough will be very sticky when it comes together!

3 Once dough has come together, shape into a ball, and place back into the bowl and cover with a slightly damp, clean towel. Let rise for 30–40 minutes, until dough has doubled in size.

4 Punch down the dough once it has doubled and divide it into 12 equal pieces. Grease a cast iron skillet with coconut oil. Roll each piece of dough into a smooth, round ball and place into the skillet. Once all the dough balls are in the skillet, let it rise for another 15 minutes. Brush with remainder of the coconut oil. Bake in the preheated oven for 25 minutes, or until golden-brown.

Serve your rolls as a side to barbecue chicken!

INGREDIENTS

4 cups all purpose flour

1 envelope instant yeast

1 tsp. salt

½-inch fresh ginger, grated

½ cup pineapple juice

½ cup coconut oil, melted (plus extra for greasing)

¼ cup coconut milk

¼ cup honey

1 tsp. pure vanilla extract

2 eggs

1 egg yolk

EL KHOBZ

MAKES: 4 LOAVES | TOTAL TIME: 1 HOUR 40 MINUTES

An easy, denser bread, el khobz is a delicious Moroccan disc-like flatbread that is made primarily with semolina. Khobz, in Arabic, literally translates as "bread," so it's safe to say that it's a staple at meals; it is served with curries, tagines, zallouk, and even with relishes and jams. Most Moroccans prefer khobz to the plain white bread (made only with flour) that is eaten all over the world because of the taste of the spices and semolina. Anise seed is also often used to flavor the bread for special occasions.

INGREDIENTS

- 1 cup warm water
- 2½ Tbsp. coconut oil, plus extra for greasing
- 2 tsp. yeast
- 1½ tsp. sea salt
- 2 cups semolina
- 1¾ cups whole wheat flour
- pinch of cumin
- 4 sprigs fresh thyme, stripped

DIRECTIONS

1. Grease one large baking sheet with coconut oil. Preheat oven to 400 degrees. In a small bowl, whisk together water, coconut oil, and yeast. Sprinkle in the salt. Set the yeast mixture aside for 10 minutes, until frothy.

2. In a mixer or food processor, pulse semolina until it becomes a flour-like consistency. Add to a large bowl, and sift in whole wheat flour and cumin. Pour in wet ingredients and mix with a rubber spatula. Once dough starts to come together, turn out onto a lightly floured surface and knead until smooth. Dough should not be tacky. Add more flour if dough is sticky. Knead in stripped thyme leaves.

3. Divide dough into four equal parts and knead into balls. Leave each dough ball on the floured surface covered with a clean towel. Let dough balls rise for 30-40 minutes until doubled in size.

4. Once dough balls have risen, flatten into 5-inch discs and place each on the baking sheet. Use a sharp knife and slice an "X" through each disc. Bake for 20 minutes in the preheated oven until light brown.

Serve khobz in slices with any spicy curry.

ROSEMARY AND THYME FOCACCIA BREAD

YIELDS: 1 ROUND LOAF | TOTAL TIME: 1 HOUR 40 MINUTES

Focaccia bread is a beloved Northern Italian flatbread that is covered with all kinds of vegetable toppings. Focaccia bread has roots in Mediterranean cuisine, and is traditionally dimpled to combat the air bubbles that rise to the surface during baking. Early versions of the bread were cooked over fire-heated tiles. True to Mediterranean cuisine, olive oil is usually a main ingredient in making this bread. However, other oils can be used. Over the years, the preparation of focaccia bread has changed to accommodate the tastes of those who make it; sun dried tomatoes, onions, and olives are all common toppings. It is such a popular bread that other cultures have adopted similar versions of flatbread with different names; fougasse, fugazza, hogazza are all names of bread that have a similar composition to focaccia.

DIRECTIONS

1 Grease an 8- or 9- inch round cake pan with coconut oil and set aside. In a small bowl, mix water, yeast, and sugar together until yeast has completely dissolved in the warm water. Set aside for 10 minutes, until frothy.

2 In a larger bowl, sift together flour, salt, thyme, chili powder, and pepper. Create a well in the middle of the dry ingredients and pour the yeast mixture in. Use a rubber spatula to mix the dry and wet ingredients together. Start kneading the dough together until smooth. If the dough is too sticky, add in a little extra flour.

3 Set dough in the bowl and cover with a clean towel to rise for 20 minutes. Add in coconut oil and chopped rosemary and knead again for 2-3 minutes until rosemary and oil are evenly distributed. Set dough back in the bowl and rise for another 40 minutes.

4 Punch down dough and press dough down into greased cake pan. Preheat oven to 400 degrees and place the cake pan nearby to allow one last rise of 15 minutes near the hot oven. Use a serrated knife to slice into the dough in a pattern.

5 Brush the top of the dough with coconut oil and sprinkle extra sea salt and rosemary on top. Bake in preheated oven for 25 minutes.

Serve focaccia plain or as a side.

INGREDIENTS

1 cup lukewarm water

2¼ Tbsp. instant yeast

pinch of cane sugar

3 cups all purpose flour, sifted

1 tsp. coarse sea salt, plus extra to garnish

1 tsp. of dried thyme

½ tsp. of chili powder

pepper

2 Tbsp. coconut oil, plus extra for brushing

1 sprig of fresh rosemary, de-stemmed and chopped

SAMOAN PANI POPO

MAKES: 12 BUNS | TOTAL TIME: 40 MINUTES

Considering that "Popo" means coconut and "pani" means "buns" in Samoan, this delicious coconut sauce soaked bread has a name that's quite literal. These buns may resemble a regular dinner roll, but the light coconutty flavor is unlike any other bread. Traditionally, the coconut milk is sweetened, and then poured over the bread to create a glaze. It is considered to be a dessert, but is also served as a side to poultry. The Pacific Islanders have extensive access to coconut, so it's a main ingredient in many of their dishes.

INGREDIENTS

- 1½ cup coconut milk, divided
- ¼ cup warm water
- 2 tsp. instant yeast
- 3 Tbsp. coconut oil, plus extra for greasing
- 4 Tbsp. honey
- ¼ cup non fat milk powder
- 1 large egg
- 1 tsp. salt
- 4 cups all purpose flour

DIRECTIONS

1. Grease your cast iron skillet with coconut oil. In a small bowl, combine 1 cup of the coconut milk (warmed), warm water, and yeast. Set aside for 5-10 minutes until frothy.

2. In a large bowl, add in melted coconut oil, honey, powdered milk, egg, and salt. Whisk it together vigorously. Pour in frothy yeast mixture into the large bowl with the egg mixture and whisk again, making sure to combine the ingredients thoroughly.

3. Preheat your oven to 350 degrees. Sift in flour and mix with a rubber spatula to combine. Once the dough comes together, turn out onto a floured surface and knead for 5-6 minutes until dough is elastic. Divide into 12 pieces and roll into balls.

4. Place the 12 dough balls in the greased skillet and set aside for 30 minutes to rest and rise. Brush the tops of the unbaked buns with some of the remaining coconut milk and then pour the rest into the bottom of the skillet. Bake for 20 minutes in the preheated oven.

Serve each pani popo as a side to grilled chicken or barbecued vegetables.

SESAME TOPPED CHALLAH BREAD

YIELDS: 1 LOAF | TOTAL TIME: 2 HOURS

Challah bread is a braided loaf that has a rich history. Dating back to the 15th century, food historians have noted that the first mentions of challah bread were in Austria—where there was a large Jewish population. Today, challah is the ritual bread of Jewish tradition and is common across multiple countries in Europe. The word challah comes from the Hebrew word for "portion." The arms of the braided challah are meant to symbolize the intertwining arms of love, peace, friendship, justice, and truth.

DIRECTIONS

1. In a large bowl, combine warm water and yeast. Mix together and set aside for 5 minutes until the mixture begins to foam. Mix in honey, coconut oil, and salt and whisk thoroughly. Reserve three tablespoons of the whisked eggs for the egg wash. Add in the remaining eggs.
2. Fold in four cups of flour, one cup at a time and mix until dough comes together. Dough will be sticky. Turn out onto a floured surface and knead until smooth (it will still be slightly moist).
3. Oil the same large bowl used to mix the dough and place the kneaded dough inside. Cover with a clean towel and set aside in a warm place for an hour.
4. Once dough has doubled in size, punch the dough down and knead again on the floured surface. Repeat step 3. Preheat your oven to 375 degrees.
5. Cut dough into 6 equal parts and roll into long ropes. Braid according to the diagram below. Place on a greased cookie sheet. Mix the egg reserved for the egg wash with 1 tablespoon of water. Brush the loaf liberally with half the egg wash. Top with sesame seeds if desired.
6. Bake in preheated oven for 15 minutes until golden brown. Remove from the oven, brush with remaining egg wash, and return to the oven for an additional 15 minutes.

Serve your challah bread as a side to soups, curries, or simply brushed with jam or other sandwich spreads.

INGREDIENTS

- 1 cup warm water
- 2½ tsp. instant yeast
- ⅓ cup honey
- ¼ cup coconut oil, melted (plus extra for greasing)
- 1 tsp. salt
- 3 eggs, whisked and divided
- 4½ cups white bread flour
- 1 Tbsp. water
- sesame seeds, to garnish (optional)

SOFT GARLIC WHOLE WHEAT PRETZELS

MAKES: 6 MEDIUM SIZED PRETZELS | TOTAL TIME: 40 MINUTES

The origin of pretzels is mysterious–this twisted bread has strong ties to the Catholic religion. The shape of a pretzel was rumored to have emerged in 610 AD somewhere in Europe–most food historians suggest that it emerged in a monastery in France or Italy. In fact, the pretzels were apparently used to entice children to memorize biblical versus and prayers. The shape of the pretzel was said to be a child's folded, praying arms. Another theory is that the pretzel took the shape of the Christian Trinity.

DIRECTIONS

1 Line two baking trays with parchment paper and preheat oven to 400 degrees.

2 In a small bowl, whisk together warm water, yeast, sugar, and sea salt. Set aside for 10 minutes, until mixture is frothy. In a large bowl, sift the whole wheat flour and then add in coconut oil and the yeast mixture. Use your hands to knead until dough pulls away from the bowl.

3 Dump dough onto a floured surface and knead again. Dough should be elastic. Replace the dough ball in the bowl and cover with a clean cloth. Let the dough rise for 20-60 minutes until doubled. Divide dough into six equal parts and roll each into a long rope measuring approximately 16-18 inches.

4 On the stove, bring 5 cups of water to a boil and dissolve the baking soda in the water. Fold each rope into a pretzel shape and lower (with a spatula) into the boiling mixture of water and baking soda. Leave for 30 seconds, and use the spatula to remove the pretzel, letting the excess water drain through the slots of the spatula and place it on one of the two prepared baking sheets. Repeat for each dough rope.

5 In a small bowl, whisk together the egg and the 2 tablespoons of water. Use a pastry brush to liberally brush each pretzel with the egg wash. Garnish each with minced garlic and sea salt. Bake in the preheated oven for 15 minutes, or until beautifully browned.

Serve each pretzel hot with cheese dip or plain!

INGREDIENTS

- 1 ½ cup warm water
- 2 Tbsp. yeast
- 1 Tbsp. brown sugar
- 1 Tbsp. coarse sea salt, plus more to garnish
- 4 cups of whole wheat flour, plus more for kneading
- ¼ cup room temperature coconut oil
- 5 cups of water
- ¼ cup baking soda
- 1 egg
- 2 Tbsp. of water
- ½ Tbsp. minced garlic

TURKISH SIMIT

SERVES: 5 | TOTAL TIME: 1 HOUR 15 MINUTES

Turkish Simit is the ancestor of everyone's favorite breakfast bread: the bagel. The delicious twisted bread is actually Turkey's national food, and very popular throughout Middle Eastern countries (although it is recognized by different names). Simit is dipped in a glaze of honey and covered with toasted sesame seeds. Simit dates back to the early 1400s during the Ottoman Empire. Simit was food for the masses and was consumed both by the nobility and the laborers in Turkey. In fact, it's so popular in Europe that it's made appearances in artist's paintings and popular poetry. Warwick Goble's oil painting "the Simit Seller" is one such example.

DIRECTIONS

1 In a small bowl, whisk together water, sugar, yeast, and coconut oil. In a larger bowl, sift in whole wheat flour and salt.

2 Add wet ingredients to dry ingredients. Divide the mixture in three equal parts while using a rubber spatula to mix the dough together. Spread ½ teaspoon coconut oil over the dough and knead the dough within the bowl until it comes together. Dough should be slightly tacky. If the dough is too dry, add in a tablespoon of water at a time until the consistency is correct. Leave the dough in the bowl, oil the sides with some melted coconut oil, cover it with a clean towel, and let the dough rise for an hour.

3 Dump out the dough onto a lightly floured surface and divide it into 5 parts. Roll each dough section out into a long, thin rope (about ½-inch in width). Fold each rope in half, twist the length, and shape into a ring. Press the ends of the twisted rope together. The middle of the ring will be much larger than a regular bagel ring.

4 In another small bowl, whisk together the ¼ cup of water and the honey. Pour the sesame seeds in a shallow dish. Brush the top of each simit liberally with the mixture of honey and water. Press the brushed top of each simit into the dish of sesame seeds. Place each simit about 1-inch away from the next. Bake for 20 minutes in the preheated oven, until evenly golden-brown.

Serve simit warmed or like a bagel, with cream cheese and turkey slices.

INGREDIENTS

- 1 cup warm water
- 1 Tbsp. turbinado sugar
- 1 Tbsp. yeast
- 2 heaping Tbsp. coconut oil, plus extra for greasing
- 2½ cups whole wheat flour
- 1 tsp. pink Himalayan salt
- ¼ cup water
- 3 Tbsp. honey
- 1 cup of toasted sesame seeds

SOUP'S ON

FRENCH ONION SOUP

SERVES: 5 | TOTAL TIME: 40 MINUTES

Onion soups have always been popular–the powerful onion flavor always releases a warming magic. French onion soup, however, was an 18th century creation in France. Traditionally, French onion soup contains white wine but can also be made "kid" friendly. The myths surrounding French onion soup say that King Louis XV and his family served one of the first versions of French Onion soup out of necessity–there was a serious lack of ingredients in the pantry!

DIRECTIONS

1. In a large pot, heat the coconut oil over medium heat. Add the onions to the pot and saute for 20 minutes, until the onions have evenly browned and cooked down. Add the garlic and flour and cook for another minute.
2. Add beef stock, vegetable broth, and Worcestershire sauce. Mix well and bring to a boil. Add in two sprigs of thyme. Lower the heat and cover for 2-3 minutes.
3. Add in cayenne pepper and salt and stir. Cook over low heat for another minute or so and remove from heat. Place 5 ovenproof soup bowls on an oven sheet and ladle soup into the bowls. Place two slices of baguette in each bowl (they will float), and sprinkle cheese evenly over the soup.
4. Set your oven to broil and broil until cheese bubbles (2-3 minutes).

Serve your French onion soup hot from the oven garnished with fresh sprigs of thyme.

INGREDIENTS

- 1 Tbsp. coconut oil
- 3 large Spanish onions or yellow onions, diced
- 4 cloves garlic, minced
- 1 Tbsp. all purpose flour
- 3 cups beef stock
- ¼ cup vegetable broth
- 1 tsp. Worcestershire sauce
- 3 sprigs of thyme, divided
- 1 tsp. cayenne pepper
- ½ tsp. salt
- 1 baguette, sliced into 1-inch thick slices
- ½ cup low fat Gruyere cheese, grated

HUNGARIAN MUSHROOM SOUP

SERVES: 6 | TOTAL TIME: 50 MINUTES

Hungarian Mushroom soup is creamy and bursting with flavor. A relatively recent invention, the soup is a popular dish at many restaurants in Budapest. It is also a popular dish on Hungarian dinner tables, served with dense bread and a dollop of sour cream. The addition of Hungarian paprika gives it the trademark flavor that is so popular. It is now available to purchase as a dry soup mix!

DIRECTIONS

1 In a large pot, heat coconut oil. Add in onion and mushrooms and saute over medium heat for at least 10 minutes (until the juices of the mushrooms and onions release). Reduce heat to low.

2 In a small bowl, whisk together flour and sweet paprika. Add to the pot and stir to combine mushrooms, onions, and the flour mixture. Pour in chicken broth, milk, and tomato sauce. Increase heat to medium high and stir while simmering. Simmer for 20 minutes. Soup will thicken.

3 Set the heat to lowest setting and pour in lemon juice, Greek yogurt or sour cream, and parsley. Stir over low heat for 5-6 minutes..

Serve this soup with freshly chopped parsley and extra sour cream or Greek yogurt with a side of crusty bread.

INGREDIENTS

1 Tbsp. coconut oil

1 large Spanish onion, finely diced

1 pound of cremini mushrooms, sliced

1 Tbsp. cayenne powder

¼ cup flour

1 Tbsp. sweet paprika

3 cups of chicken broth

1 cup skim milk

2 Tbsp. tomato sauce

½ cup Greek yogurt or sour cream

juice of 1 lemon

1 Tbsp. chopped parsley

VEGETABLE MISO SOUP

SERVES: 3 | TOTAL TIME: 45 MINUTES

A Japanese staple, Miso soup is a very flavorful broth with vegetables and noodles that is nourishing and warm. Miso paste is made from fermented soy bean and the fungus Aspergillus oryzae, known in Japanese as kōjikin. Using Miso paste (mashed soybeans) was an age-old tradition for the Japanese nobility that dated as far back as the 8th century. It slowly became more popular with the common people from the 17th to the 19th century when the State encouraged its citizens to eat and live more frugally with the "austerity ordinance." It quickly became very popular, and continued on as a delicacy of Japan.

DIRECTIONS

1. In a medium pot, bring water to a boil over medium high heat. In a small bowl, combine chicken broth, miso paste, oyster sauce, and soy sauce.
2. Pour the mixture into the water and stir. Let the mixture come back up to a boil, and then add in the white pepper and chili flakes. Stir to combine. Add in udon noodles and boil for 1 minute.
3. Add in the mushrooms and spinach and reduce heat to low. Stir for a few minutes until spinach has wilted and mushrooms are cooked. Garnish with chopped green onions.

Serve your miso soup piping hot.

INGREDIENTS

- 3 cups water
- ⅛ cup chicken broth
- 2 Tbsp. white miso paste
- ½ tsp. oyster sauce
- ½ tsp. soy sauce
- ¼ tsp. white pepper
- ½ tsp. chili pepper flakes
- 7 oz. udon noodles
- 1 cup oyster mushrooms
- ½ cup fresh baby spinach
- 2 green onions, chopped

CLASSIC VICHYSSOISE

SERVES: 6 | TOTAL TIME: 50 MINUTES

Vichyssoise is a classic, cold leek and potato soup. A common myth about why it's eaten cold: King Louis XV, in the 1700s, enjoyed eating potato soup, but was known for being a little paranoid about being poisoned. He had multiple people taste his food before he ate anything to ensure that nothing nefarious was going on. By the time his potato soup reached him, it was cold so it became a soup that was commonly eaten cold. The addition of leek with the potatoes was an invention of the early 1900s for whom Chef Louis Diat is responsible. He worked at the Ritz Carlton in Paris, and was looking for a soup to cool his guests down in the hot summers of France.

DIRECTIONS

1. In a large pot, heat coconut oil and then add in onions. Cook until onions are lightly browned. Add in leeks and cook until softened.
2. Add in potatoes, sea salt, pepper and allspice. Cook for 2-3 minutes. Pour in vegetable broth. Bring to a boil and continue to stir. Test the potatoes by sticking a fork in one of the pieces. Once the potatoes slide off the fork, they're cooked.
3. Pour in the milk and bring to a boil once more. Turn the heat off and let the soup cool slightly. Using an immersion blender, blend the ingredients together until a thick, creamy soup forms.

Serve your vichyssoise topped with croutons, chives, and a side of baguettes.

INGREDIENTS

1 Tbsp. coconut oil

1 large Spanish onion, diced

6 large leeks, rinsed and chopped into rounds

2 large potatoes, peeled and diced

8 cups vegetable broth

½ tsp. sea salt

½ tsp. pepper

¼ tsp. allspice

½ cup milk

chives, to garnish

MAISON ORPH
FOR ENERGIZING COOKING
POUR UNE CUISINE ÉNERGISANTE
ORGANIC
BIOLOGIQUE
Raw Virgin Coconut Oil
Huile de noix de coco vierge crue
850 g (30 oz)

THE VEGETARIAN'S TABLE

CORN AND SPANISH RICE EMPANADAS

SERVES: 6 | TOTAL TIME: 1 HOUR 25 MINUTES

South American restaurants and home kitchens are famous for their delicious empanadas that can be filled with virtually any savory mix on the planet. Traditionally, empanadas are filled with spiced meat and vegetables. Empanadas are said to have originated from Spain; however, South American countries have perfected the art of the empanada. The name comes from the Spanish word "empanar" which means "to coat with bread."

DIRECTIONS

1 Preheat your oven to 375 degrees. In a large pot, bring vegetable broth to a boil. Add in brown rice and a ½ tablespoon of coconut oil. Cover and stir intermittently for 45 minutes. In a separate skillet, heat the other ½ tablespoon of coconut oil and sauté onion and garlic until garlic has browned and onion is translucent. Pour crushed tomatoes into the skillet and simmer.

2 Add crushed tomato mixture to the pot with the cooked rice and mix thoroughly on medium heat. Add in pepper, cumin, paprika, salt and corn kernels. Stir until all the liquid has evaporated and set aside to cool.

3 Roll out thawed pie crust and use a 5-inch round cookie cutter to cut out circles from the crust. Add 1 tablespoon of rice and corn to the middle of each pie crust circle. Fold the circles in half and press seams together. To make the braided border, stagger the folds of the edge of the pie crust underneath each fold.

4 Place each empanada on a parchment lined baking tray. Whisk together the egg and 1 teaspoon water and brush each empanada liberally with the egg wash. Place each empanada 2-inches apart and bake for 25 minutes in preheated oven.

Serve your empanadas hot from the oven with a fresh squeeze of lime juice.

INGREDIENTS

2 cups vegetable broth

½ cup long grain brown rice

1 Tbsp. coconut oil, divided

½ red onion, diced

1 clove garlic, minced

½ cup crushed tomatoes

¼ tsp. ground pepper

¼ tsp. cumin

½ tsp. paprika

¼ tsp. salt

1 ½ cup canned corn kernels

1 9-inch premade pie crust, thawed

1 egg

1 tsp. water

lime juice, to garnish

CRISPY FALAFEL

SERVES: 6 | TOTAL TIME: 30 MINUTES

This is another quintessentially Middle Eastern dish with unclear origins. Because it's so delicious, many countries want to claim the responsibility for the creation of this great vegetarian dish. This speaks to historical disputes over territory and culture and history—but it's incredible to note that the flavors and traditions from Israel and Palestine have created a culinary delight that people all over the world love. Wherever it originated, we can all agree that we're glad it exists.

INGREDIENTS

- 1 can chickpeas, washed, rinsed and dried
- ¼ cup curly parsley, chopped
- ¼ cup cilantro, chopped
- ¼ cup all purpose flour
- 4 cloves garlic
- juice of ½ a lemon
- 2 Tbsp. breadcrumbs
- 1 tsp. salt
- ½ tsp. cumin
- ½ tsp. coriander powder
- ¼ tsp. cayenne pepper
- pinch of black pepper
- ¼ cup coconut oil

DIRECTIONS

1. Add all the ingredients except for the coconut oil into a food processor and pulse until paste-like mixture forms. Transfer mixture into a bowl and cover with plastic wrap in the fridge. Rest for 30 minutes.

2. Heat coconut oil in a skillet. Form a 1½-inch ball with the falafel batter and shallow fry for 2 minutes on one side. Flip them over with a spatula and cook for another 2-3 minutes. Repeat for rest of the batter.

Serve your falafel inside a pita with tzatziki and fresh lettuce.

GNOCCHI IN TOMATO SAGE SAUCE

SERVES: 4 | TOTAL TIME: 30 MINUTES

Italy, the land of pasta, has yielded some of the most popular dishes in the world. Most people believe that the word gnocchi comes from the Italian word "nocca", which means knuckles–an apt name for the interestingly shaped dough balls! Gnocchi's main ingredient, of course, is potato. Although variations of gnocchi popped up in the late 15th century, cooking with potatoes was introduced to the Italians two centuries later by the Spanish explorers that returned from South America with a few culinary tricks.

DIRECTIONS

FOR THE GNOCCHI

1 Preheat your oven to 350 degrees, and bake four potatoes for 50–60 minutes (or until done). (Tip: Pierce your potatoes with a fork so they cook faster.) Peel the potatoes as soon as they are cool enough to handle. Grate the potatoes into a bowl and mix in the egg (mixture should still be warm). Turn out the mixture onto a floured surface (use 4 tablespoons of flour on your surface) and add in the remainder of the flour. Knead with your hands and form a dough-like mixture. Roll out into a rope-shape that is about ½-inch thick and cut dough into 1-inch pieces. If making the signature lines, roll on a gnocchi board or press a floured fork into the dough to make an impression. Continue onto step 2.

IF USING STORE-BOUGHT GNOCCHI

2 Boil water in a large pot and drop in store bought or homemade gnocchi. Boil until gnocchi is cooked and floats to the top. This will take about 40 seconds. Use a slotted spoon to drain the water from the cooked gnocchi and transfer to a separate bowl.

TO MAKE THE SAUCE

3 Heat the coconut oil in a saucepan and sauté garlic until lightly browned. Pour in tomato sauce and simmer on low heat. Add in the rest of the ingredients. Mash the diced tomatoes within the sauce and continue until sauce is without chunks. Simmer for 2–3 more minutes.

4 Pour the tomato sauce onto the bottom of a casserole dish or cast iron skillet. Layer the cooked gnocchi on top and toss lightly in the base of tomato sauce. You may sprinkle any extra cheese on top of the dish.

5 Broil on high for 5–10 minutes or until cheese and sauce darken. Garnish with sage leaves and grated parmesan, if desired.

INGREDIENTS

FOR THE GNOCCHI

2 16 oz. packages store-bought gnocchi or 4 medium russet potatoes

2 cups all purpose flour

2 eggs, beaten

FOR THE SAUCE

1 Tbsp. coconut oil

3 cloves garlic, minced

1 cup tomato sauce

2 cups of Italian seasoned, diced tomatoes

¼ cup chicken or vegetable broth

¼ cup shredded cheese (mozzarella or cheddar), plus extra to garnish

1 tsp. grated parmesan (optional)

½ tsp. oregano

¼ tsp. onion powder

½ Tbsp. ground pepper

2 leaves of sage, plus extra to garnish

JAPCHAE: KOREAN GLASS NOODLE STIR FRY

SERVES: 4 | TOTAL TIME: 35 MINUTES

Glass noodles are a particularly enticing part of Korean culinary history. Japchae was a creation of the 17th century, and surprisingly didn't contain meat or noodles like the modern day version. In fact, japchae is the Korean word for "vegetables," and that is what the original dish was comprised of, like most 17th century Korean meals. It was first created for royalty by a palace cook. The flavors became popular, and today, japchae is served with vegetables or meat–but the glass noodles are the main event.

DIRECTIONS

1. Cook the noodles according to package instructions (boil in water for 5-6 minutes and then rinse with cold water to prevent sticking together).
2. Mix together all the ingredients for the sauce in a small bowl and set aside.
3. Heat coconut oil in a large wok and sauté onion, ginger, and garlic for 1 minute. Add in spinach and mushrooms and continue to cook.
4. Pour in half of the sauce and cook for 1 minute. Add in the noodles and the remainder of the sauce and toss on high heat for a few minutes until noodles are coated in the sauce and vegetables are evenly dispersed.

Serve each Japchae garnished with fresh green onions and toasted sesame seeds.

INGREDIENTS

8¾ oz. of sweet potato starch noodles (Myun Dang)

FOR THE SAUCE

1/3 cup soy sauce

1 Tbsp. rice vinegar

½ Tbsp. chili pepper flakes

2 tsp. brown sugar

1 tsp. ketchup

1 clove garlic, minced

FOR THE STIR FRY

½ tablespoon coconut oil

1 small onion, diced

2 cloves garlic, minced

1-inch fresh ginger, grated

3 cups of spinach

8 white mushrooms

2 green onions, sliced for garnish

sesame seeds, to garnish

MUSHROOM AND RED ONION LASAGNA

SERVES: 6-7 | TOTAL TIME: 1 HOUR AND 30 MINUTES

Lasagna is a classic Italian comfort food: layers of fresh, savory tomato sauce and different cheeses bind the ruffled pasta together to become a favorite at most dinner tables. The earliest mention of the lasagna noodle was traced back to the Ancient Greeks; their word for the long strips of dough was laganon; however, after the Romans invaded, the tradition of layering pasta, sauce and cheese became an Italian specialty perfected in Naples.

DIRECTIONS

1 Spray a casserole dish with cooking spray and preheat your oven to 375 degrees. In a large pot, heat coconut oil. Add onion, garlic, and chili pepper flakes. Cook until garlic browns and onion turns translucent. Then, add in sliced mushrooms and cook for 1 minute.

2 Pour in crushed tomatoes and vegetable broth and stir to combine. Bring mixture to a boil.

3 Sprinkle in oregano, pepper, and basil. While stirring, pour in lemon juice. Simmer for 5 minutes, cover, and set aside.

4 In a medium bowl, beat the egg and mix with ricotta and parsley. For extra spice, add in a pinch of cayenne pepper.

5 Spread a thin layer of the sauce on the bottom of your greased casserole dish. Layer three cooked lasagna noodles on top. For the next layer, spread a third of your ricotta cheese mixture over the noodles and sprinkle ½ cup of mozzarella/cheddar shredded cheese on top. Lay three more lasagna noodles on top (trim noodles to fit dish if necessary). Add ⅓ of the remaining sauce on top, and sprinkle another ½ cup of shredded cheese on top of this layer. Repeat this pattern from the first layer of noodles onwards, until your last three noodles are placed, and you add the last layer of sauce and shredded cheese on top.

6 Bake your lasagna uncovered for 25 minutes in the preheated oven.

Slice the hot lasagna with a sharp knife and use a spatula to lift the slices so the layers remain intact. Garnish with extra parsley.

INGREDIENTS

1 Tbsp. coconut oil

1 large red onion, diced

4 cloves of garlic, minced

½ tsp. chili pepper flakes

6 white mushrooms, sliced

1 can crushed tomatoes

¼ cup vegetable broth

1 tsp. dried oregano

1 tsp. ground pepper

2 Tbsp. fresh basil, finely chopped

juice of ½ a lemon

1 egg

2 cups ricotta cheese

2 Tbsp. parsley, plus extra to garnish

pinch of cayenne pepper (optional)

2 cups of shredded mozzarella and cheddar blend

¼ cup crumbled parmesan

12 lasagna noodles, cooked

BAKED RATATOUILLE

SERVES: 2 | TOTAL TIME: 1 HOUR 30 MINUTES

Made famous by the popular Disney movie, Ratatouille hails from Nice, France, where, long ago, it was made by farmers in that region. This colorful vegetable stew is traditionally made with the fresh summer vegetable crop. While aubergine (eggplant) was not part of the original recipe, it has become a popular addition to modern variations of Ratatouille. Quite literally, the word 'ratatouille' is an extension of its root French word "touiller" translated as "to toss food."

DIRECTIONS

1 Using a mandoline slicer or sharp knife, slice eggplants, zucchini, tomato, and red onion into 1⁄16-inch slices. Preheat oven to 375 degrees and set aside an ovenproof casserole dish.

2 In a saucepan, heat coconut oil and add in garlic. When it starts to brown, add in crushed tomatoes, vegetable broth, and roasted red pepper. Simmer for 2–3 minutes while stirring. Add in basil, oregano and paprika and stir to combine.

3 Spread ladlefuls of the sauce onto the bottom of your casserole pan. Add in alternating thin slices of vegetables and layer in rows. Brush coconut oil over the vegetables and sprinkle with pepper. Cover dish with aluminum foil and bake in preheated oven for 40 minutes. Uncover and bake for an additional 15 minutes.

Serve your ratatouille on the side of a main dish or use a bigger serving as a great vegetarian main course.

INGREDIENTS

2 long eggplants

2 zucchini

1 roma tomato

¼ red onion

1 Tbsp. coconut oil, plus extra for brushing

1 clove garlic, minced

1 cup crushed tomatoes

¼ cup vegetable broth

1 roasted red pepper, diced

½ tsp. chili pepper flakes

1 tsp. basil, chopped

¼ tsp. dried oregano

½ tsp. smoked paprika

pepper to taste

SHAKSHUKA

SERVES: 4 | TOTAL TIME: 48 MINUTES

The earliest origin stories of shakshuka emerge from the Ottoman Empire in Turkey; the modern versions however, are attributed to North African countries that added the spicy flavors. Specifically in Tunisia, eggs were an important protein for African-Jewish cooking (many Jewish immigrants settled in North Africa). Shakshuka was a stew that didn't contain meat so that Jewish families could adhere to their religious diets. Part of the appeal (other than the taste), was the affordability of the ingredients, especially when many of the North African Jewish families immigrated to Israel. The struggling families found it easy to pay for and prepare Shakshuka; a word that means "all mixed up." Israeli shakshuka yields the version we know best (poached eggs in a tomato stew).

DIRECTIONS

1 Preheat your oven to 375 degrees. Heat coconut oil in a skillet. Sauté onion and garlic until onions are translucent. Add in red and yellow peppers and reduce to low heat.

2 Add in red chili flakes, pepper, salt, paprika, and cumin, and stir to evenly disperse. Pour in diced tomatoes. Simmer on low heat while intermittently stirring for 10-12 minutes. Sauce will thicken.

3 Transfer the sauce to an ovenproof casserole dish. Create four wells in the sauce, evenly spaced. Crack each egg into a well. Carefully transfer the casserole dish to the oven and bake for 10 minutes until the egg whites have set. Garnish with ground pepper.

Serve shakshuka with warm bread and garnished with cilantro.

INGREDIENTS

1 Tbsp. coconut oil

3 shallots, diced

2 cloves of garlic, minced

1 red pepper, roughly chopped

1 yellow pepper, roughly chopped

1 can (28 ounces) diced tomatoes

1 Tbsp. red chili flakes

1 tsp. pepper, plus extra to garnish

1 tsp. sea salt

1 tsp. sweet paprika

1 tsp. cumin

4 whole eggs

cilantro, to garnish

VEGETABLE PAD-THAI

SERVES: 4 | TOTAL TIME: 45 MINUTES

We know that Thailand is credited with pad-thai, and it's the consensus that pad-thai was a recent, 1930s invention and became so popular that it's very commonly sold as street food in Thailand's small villages and other tourist destinations. The original name of pad thai was "kway teow phat Thai" in a Chinese dialect. The very idea of stir frying rice noodles was an idea that immigrated to Thailand from China. The addition of peanuts, red chilies, tamarind, and other flavors came from the minds of Thai natives.

DIRECTIONS

1 Cook rice noodles according to package instructions and drain. In a small bowl, mix together soy sauce, rice vinegar, lime juice, and honey and set aside.

2 In a large wok, heat 2 tablespoons of coconut oil. Add in ginger and garlic, when they are browned, add in red pepper and carrots and sauté for 2 minutes. Add in green onion and chili flakes and oyster sauce (if using). Pour in half of the sauce mixture and sauté for another minute.

3 Add cooked noodles to the wok and mix thoroughly so that vegetables and sauce are evenly distributed. Add in remaining sauce and cook for 2-3 minutes.

Serve your pad thai topped with crushed, roasted peanuts and fresh cilantro.

INGREDIENTS

16 oz. rice noodles

FOR THE SAUCE

¼ cup soy sauce

2 Tbsp. rice vinegar

2 Tbsp. lime juice

1 Tbsp. honey

FOR THE STIR FRY

2 Tbsp. coconut oil

2 cloves garlic, minced

1 Tbsp. fresh ginger, grated

1 red pepper, sliced

1 cup matchstick carrots

½ cup green onions

½ tsp. chili pepper flakes

1 Tbsp. oyster sauce (optional)

crushed peanut, to garnish

cilantro, to garnish

ZALLOUK EGGPLANT CURRY

SERVES: 2 | TOTAL TIME: 1 HOUR

This traditional Moroccan recipe combines the smoky flavors of aubergines, tomatoes, and a myriad of aromatic spices. Locals refer to it as an eggplant salad, but this salad is different than the regular salad we've come to know in North America. This is more like a dip or a spread that is generally served with dense breads, pitas, or as a side to a meatier main dish.

DIRECTIONS

1 Grease a large baking sheet with half a tablespoon of coconut oil. Cut the peeled eggplant into ½-inch rounds. Brush each slice of eggplant with another ½ tablespoon of coconut oil. Heat your oven to 375 degrees and bake for 30-35 minutes until eggplants have browned.

2 While eggplants are roasting in the oven, heat the remainder of the coconut oil in a skillet over low heat. Add in garlic and salt and sauté until the garlic is fragrant. Add in chopped tomato and sauté until tomatoes are soft, but still hold their shape. Remove eggplant from the oven and cool it on the counter before chopping into small pieces.

3 Add in tomato sauce, paprika, cumin, pepper, and coriander. Cover and simmer for 3-5 minutes, stirring intermittently. Add in eggplant and cook while stirring for another 2-3 minutes. Add lemon juice and chopped cilantro. Simmer for a few minutes before removing from heat.

Serve zallouk with a side of denser bread, garnished with fresh cilantro and an extra squeeze of lemon.

INGREDIENTS

2 Tbsp. of coconut oil, divided

1 large eggplant, peeled

2 cloves of garlic

1 tsp. sea salt

1 tomato, chopped

½ cup of tomato sauce

1½ tsp. smoked paprika

1 tsp. cumin

½ tsp. pepper

¼ tsp. ground coriander

juice of half a lemon

½ cup of chopped cilantro

CARNIVAL OF THE CARNIVORES

THE ALL-AMERICAN BURGER

SERVES: 2 | TOTAL TIME: 30 MINUTES

The burger, an all-American staple food that combines carbs, protein, dairy, and fresh veggies all in one fell swoop! Although there are stories and theories about ground meat being consumed in Asia by the Mongols, the hamburger concept (two buns and a ground beef patty) we have all come to know and love originates in America where, for the glory, many an establishment have claimed that they served "the first" classic hamburger - and some of these stories date back to the 1900s. Diners and sandwich shops in Connecticut, Ohio, and New York have all laid claim to the title.

DIRECTIONS

1 In a large bowl, thoroughly combine all ingredients with a rubber spatula. Cover the bowl with plastic wrap and let marinate for 5-10 minutes.

2 Divide meat into two parts and shape two patties with your hands (they will be thick patties). Heat a skillet on the cooktop to medium high and place one patty on the skillet. Cook on the heat for 3 minutes and use a spatula to flip over. Repeat this process until the burger has browned on both sides and cooked through to your preference. Place two slices of cheese over the finished burger and let them melt before taking the burger off the heat. Repeat with the second patty.

Serve your burgers on sesame topped hamburger buns with lettuce and tomatoes.

INGREDIENTS

½ pound of extra lean ground beef

¼ cup breadcrumbs

¼ cup fresh cilantro, chopped (optional)

1 egg

2 Tbsp. tomato sauce

½ Tbsp. lemon juice

1 tsp. chili pepper flakes

1 tsp. garlic, minced

1 tsp. coconut oil

½ tsp. onion powder

¼ tsp. pepper

¼ tsp. oregano

TOPPINGS

4 slices of marbled American Cheddar cheese

4 sesame topped burger buns

2 leaves of romaine lettuce

2 slices of tomatoes

SOUTHERN CHICKEN AND CORNBREAD WAFFLES

SERVES: 6 | TOTAL TIME: 50 MINUTES

The dynamic duo of chicken and waffles is commonly regarded as a very Southern American culinary comfort food. During the early 17th century, many cookbooks contained delicious recipes for braised chicken. By the 1800s, more variations of chicken emerged. These recipes were adapted by the African-American cooks who used breadcrumbs to coat and fry the chicken. The well cooked chicken didn't spoil easily, and was sent to soldiers on the battlefield by their wives. The waffles were added later as a sweet treat under the salty and crispy chicken.

DIRECTIONS

FOR THE WAFFLES

1 In a large bowl, sift together flour, cornmeal, baking powder, baking soda, and salt. In a separate bowl, whisk together cashew milk, coconut oil, lemon juice, and honey. Beat in egg yolks, and add the thyme leaves to the batter.

2 Whisk egg whites until frothy, with soft peaks in a separate bowl and set aside. Add egg yolk mixture to the dry ingredients and mix until just combined. Fold in egg whites and mix again. Ladle a sixth of the mixture into a greased waffle iron and cook according to waffle iron instructions. Repeat until you have six waffles.

FOR THE CHICKEN

3 Line a baking sheet with parchment paper and preheat your oven to 375 degrees. Brush the parchment with coconut oil. In a small bowl, whisk the eggs together.

4 Coat each chicken breast slice in flour, dip in egg mixture and shake off the excess, and then coat in panko crumbs. Lay each chicken breast on the prepared baking sheet and bake for 8 minutes. Use a spatula to flip them over. Bake for another 6-8 minutes.

Serve each crispy chicken breast on top of a hot waffle.

INGREDIENTS

FOR THE WAFFLES

1½ cup all purpose flour

1 cup cornmeal, finely ground

2 tsp. baking powder

1 tsp. baking soda

2 sprigs of fresh thyme

1 tsp. sea salt

2 cups plain cashew milk

3 Tbsp. coconut oil, melted

1 Tbsp. lemon juice

2 tsp. honey

2 eggs, separated

FOR THE CHICKEN

½ Tbsp. coconut oil

2 eggs

3 chicken breasts, sliced lengthwise into thin filets

1 cup of whole wheat flour

¼ tsp. baking powder

¼ tsp. cayenne pepper

½ tsp. salt

1 cup panko bread crumbs

CHICKEN TIKKA MASALA

SERVES: 2 | TOTAL TIME: 40 MINUTES

Chicken Tikka Masala combines an incredible blend of spices to make a savory and creamy tomato gravy that pairs beautifully with bite sized pieces of chicken. Although it is most commonly associated with Indian cuisine, there remains some ambiguity regarding the true origin of the curry. A popular story postulates that an emperor from thousands of years ago ordered his chef to prepare bite sized pieces of chicken without the bone because of his fear of choking. Interestingly enough, the sauce was rumored to be a product of an interaction in the 1960s, when an officer complained of his chicken being "too dry." The chef then cooked the chicken in a can of Campbell's tomato soup, thus spurring the preparation of rich, creamy tomato sauce

DIRECTIONS

1 In a large wok, heat coconut oil and add in onions, garlic, and ginger. Sauté until onions are translucent and garlic has browned.

2 Pour in pureed tomatoes and cover and simmer for 5 minutes. Meanwhile, mix together garam masala, cumin, ground coriander, smoked paprika, turmeric powder, cayenne pepper, cinnamon, and pepper in a small bowl, and set aside.

3 Uncover the wok and add in spice mixture. Stir until combined. Pour in half and half cream and simmer for 8-10 minutes while stirring. Gravy will thicken slightly.

4 Add cooked chicken into the gravy and coat and cook for 8-9 more minutes. Garnish with chopped cilantro.

Serve your Chicken Tikka Masala with a side of fluffy basmati rice or with garlic naan.

INGREDIENTS

1 Tbsp. coconut oil

2 small Spanish onions, diced

2 cloves of garlic, minced

1 Tbsp. fresh ginger, grated

1½ diced tomatoes, pureed

½ Tbsp. garam masala

1 tsp. cumin

1 tsp. ground coriander

1 tsp. smoked paprika

½ tsp. turmeric powder

½ tsp. cayenne pepper

pinch of cinnamon

pinch of pepper

½ cup half and half cream

1 pound of chicken, cut into bite sized pieces

chopped cilantro, to garnish

CORNISH PASTIES

SERVES: 2 | TOTAL TIME: 30 MINUTES

After the mention of Cornish pasties in a Harry Potter novel, the snack sparked the curiosity of the world. The modern version of Cornish pasties originate, surprisingly, from Wisconsin, in the United States. However, the ancestry of this delicious meat and vegetable medley is said to hail from the Medieval Age, in England. In fact, these meat pies even made an appearance in Chaucer's *Canterbury Tales*.

DIRECTIONS

1. In a small bowl, mix ground beef, diced carrot, red onion, breadcrumbs, coconut oil, cayenne pepper, and salt. Heat a skillet over medium high heat. Cook the ground beef and loosen it into small pieces. Grease a baking sheet with coconut oil and preheat your oven to 425 degrees.

2. Cut two 6-inch rounds of pie crust. Fill each round with half the cooked meat. Press opposite ends together to seal the pasty at the top and place each pasty on the prepared baking sheet. Brush each liberally with the whisked egg wash. Bake for 17 minutes until golden brown.

Serve your Cornish pasty hot and flaky from the oven!

INGREDIENTS

1 9-inch pie crust or homemade pie crust

½ pound ground beef

1 carrot, diced

¼ red onion, finely diced

3 Tbsp. breadcrumbs

½ Tbsp. coconut oil, plus extra for greasing

½ tsp. cayenne pepper

¼ tsp. salt

1 egg, whisked for egg wash

FOUR PEPPER CHICKEN FAJITAS

SERVES: 4 | TOTAL TIME: 30 MINUTES

From the Rio Grande Valley of Texas, flavorful fajitas emerged–it's no secret that there are very potent flavor profiles from Mexico that influence the preparation of fajitas; it's all about location, location, location! Just South of Texas lies all the bursting spices and flavors that have become such a staple in American food. The flavors hopped right over the Texas-Mexico border to influence home cooks and restaurants!

DIRECTIONS

1. In a small bowl, make your fajita spice mixture by mixing together chili powder, cumin, paprika, Himalayan salt, coriander, chipotle chili pepper (if using), and pepper. Set aside for later use.
2. Preheat your oven to 425 degrees and spray a baking sheet with cooking spray. In one layer, spread out the peppers and onions. In a large bowl, mix together coconut oil with the fajita spice mix. Add in the strips of chicken and toss to coat with the spices and half the coconut oil.
3. Disperse the chicken strips onto the prepared pan. Drizzle the rest of the coconut oil over top of the peppers and onions. Bake in the preheated oven for 15–18 minutes.
4. On a grill pan or skillet, toast each tortilla for 30 seconds on each side.

Serve the fajitas in a toasted tortilla topped with sour cream and cilantro.

INGREDIENTS

1½ tsp. chili powder

1½ tsp. cumin

1 tsp. paprika

1 tsp. Himalayan salt

½ tsp. ground coriander

½ tsp. chipotle chili pepper (optional)

¼ tsp. ground pepper

1 Tbsp. coconut oil, melted

3 cloves of garlic, minced

3 chicken breasts, sliced

½ Spanish onion, sliced

juice of 1 lime, plus wedges for serving

4 whole peppers of different colors, sliced julienne

4 Tortillas

cilantro, to garnish

HARIYALI CHICKEN KEBABS

SERVES: 4 | TOTAL TIME: 35 MINUTES

From the kitchens of Punjab, hariyali chicken quickly established itself as one of the foremost appetizers in Indian restaurants; perhaps because of the favorite cilantro and mint combination. Hariyali chicken is traditionally made as a masala (with gravy, as a curry), but is also served in kebab form in many restaurants. The chicken is often cooked in a tandoor oven for a delicious charred, smoky taste.

DIRECTIONS

1 In a blender, pulse the cilantro, Greek yogurt, ginger, garlic, mint leaves, red chili flakes, lime juice, half the coconut oil, cayenne pepper, cumin, and salt. The result will be a runny paste. Add water in if it's too thick, or isn't blending well.

2 Transfer the cilantro mixture to a large bowl and add in the bite sized pieces of chicken. Stir to coat each piece of chicken well. Marinate in the fridge for at least 30 minutes. While the chicken is marinating, soak wooden skewers in water.

3 Heat a grill pan over medium high heat and brush with the remainder of coconut oil. Add the marinated chicken to each skewer, and place the skewers on the hot grill pan. Cook for 8-10 minutes, rotating each skewer every 45-60 seconds for an even cook of the chicken.

Serve your hariyali chicken hot with a squeeze of fresh lemon and red onions.

INGREDIENTS

¾ cup cilantro

¼ cup plain Greek yogurt

½-inch piece of fresh ginger, grated

1 clove of garlic

8 mint leaves, chopped

2 Tbsp. red chili flakes

1 Tbsp. lime juice

½ Tbsp. coconut oil, melted

1 tsp. cayenne pepper (optional)

½ tsp. cumin

¼ tsp. salt

2 Tbsp. water, if needed

2 boneless, skinless chicken breasts, cut into bite sized pieces

HULI HULI CHICKEN WITH GRILLED PINEAPPLE

SERVES: 2 | TOTAL TIME: 40 MINUTES

Hawaiians are especially proud of Huli Huli chicken, a glazed chicken that is sweet and savory at the same time. Unlike many dishes, Huli Huli chicken has a known creator, Ernest Morgado, a grill master who started making this chicken at church fundraisers and community events. As people gathered to watch Ernest create this delicious chicken, they would chant "Turn! Turn! Turn!" in Hawaiian when one side of the chicken was cooked. "Turn" in Hawaiian is "Huli", hence, the name of this tangy chicken became Huli Huli Chicken. He eventually registered it as a trademark with the state of Hawaii. As it grew in popularity, he decided to register it with the Federal government. Huli Huli chicken came into creation in the 1950s.

INGREDIENTS

- ¼ cup of sweetened pineapple juice
- 2 Tbsp. cane sugar
- 2 Tbsp. soy sauce
- 1½ Tbsp. tomato paste
- ½ Tbsp. coconut oil, melted (plus extra for greasing)
- dash of Worchester sauce
- ½-inch of fresh ginger, grated
- 2 cloves of garlic, minced
- 1 cup of pineapple, diced
- 2 chicken breasts, sliced into thin strips
- Green onions, to garnish

DIRECTIONS

1. In a small pot, whisk together pineapple juice, sugar, soy sauce, tomato paste, coconut oil, Worchester sauce, ginger, and garlic. Heat over low heat while whisking until sauce thickens, about 2–3 minutes. Cool sauce to room temperature, and reserve half the sauce in a separate bowl.
2. Marinate the chicken for at least 20 minutes. While the chicken is marinating, heat a grill pan brushed with coconut oil. Grill the pineapple slices for 2 minutes on each side. Set grilled pineapple aside.
3. Brush the grill pan with more coconut oil. Add the chicken strips to the hot grill pan and grill the chicken on the first side for 4 minutes. Use a pastry brush to brush the extra sauce on the uncooked side. Repeat for all chicken strips.
4. Flip each strip and cook for another 4 minutes. Plate the chicken with the grilled pineapple and baste the cooked chicken with the remainder of the sauce.

Serve chicken hot, garnished with fresh green onions.

JÄGERSCHNITZEL

SERVES: 2 | TOTAL TIME: 40 MINUTES

Jägerschnitzel, in German, means "Hunter's Cutlets", and was traditionally made with venison or wild boar (a hunter's game). The trademark of schnitzel is thin, pounded meat with a crispy coating. Jägerschnitzel is traditionally served with a mushroom gravy that complements the dish well. Schnitzel is the pride of Austrian restaurants; veal schnitzel (Wienerschnitzel) being the most popular of all.

DIRECTIONS

1 Preheat your oven to 375 degrees and line a baking sheet with parchment paper. Pound each pork chop to an even ¼-inch thickness with a meat mallet. Set out three shallow, open faced bowls. Add flour, pepper, and salt in one, whisked egg in another, and breadcrumbs in the last.

2 Coat each cut of pounded pork in flour, dip in egg (drip off the excess), and then coat liberally with bread crumbs. Place each cut on the prepared baking sheet. Drizzle coconut oil over each breaded pork cutlet. Bake for 8 minutes.

3 Flip each cutlet over with a spatula and baked for another 6-8 minutes until breading has browned and crisped. Remove from the oven and plate.

FOR THE MUSHROOM SAUCE

4 Heat coconut oil in a skillet. Add mushrooms and sauté until they have cooked down and released liquid. Add in beef broth, flour, and cayenne pepper. Stir the sauce constantly until thickened. This will take about 3-4 minutes. Ladle half the sauce over each pork schnitzel.

Serve your jägerschnitzel hot garnished with fresh parsley and a squeeze of lemon.

INGREDIENTS

2 boneless pork chops, pounded

½ cup all purpose flour

1 tsp. pepper

½ tsp. salt

1 egg

1 cup breadcrumbs

½ tsp. coconut oil

FOR THE MUSHROOM SAUCE

½ tsp. coconut oil

½ cup mushrooms, sliced

¼ cup beef broth

1 Tbsp. all purpose flour

½ tsp. cayenne pepper

lemon, to garnish

parsley, to garnish

BROWN RICE AND SAUSAGE JAMBALAYA

SERVES: 4 | TOTAL TIME: 50 MINUTES

In the heart of Southern Louisiana, the original European division of New Orleans (the French Quarter) produced a delicious jumble of ingredients meant to mirror the famous flavors of Spanish Paella. With the absence of certain ingredients like saffron (due to import restrictions), new spices and flavors were used. There are two distinct versions of jambalaya; Cajun and Creole–although they have similar ingredients and flavors, there are minute differences. For example, the Cajun (Arcadian-French Canadian) method of cooking jambalaya generally includes just meats like ham, chicken and pork. The Creole method uses seafood and tomatoes.

DIRECTIONS

1. Rinse your brown rice well and drain. In a large skillet, toast the brown rice for 3-4 minutes and set aside.
2. In the same skillet used to brown the rice, heat coconut oil. Add in onion, peppers, garlic, and tomato. Cook for until onions are translucent. Add in sausage rounds and cook until sausage pieces have browned (until almost cooked through).
3. Add in chicken broth, spices, and 1½ cup of water. Stir and bring to a boil. Add in crushed tomatoes. Add in toasted rice. And stir on low heat.
4. Stir for 35-40 minutes, until liquid has evaporated. Rice will still be uncooked. Add in another 1½ cup of water and stir until liquid has evaporated. Repeat with the remaining 1 cup of water. If rice is still uncooked, add in ½ a cup of water at a time until rice is tender.

Serve jambalaya hot garnished with parsley and freshly ground pepper.

INGREDIENTS

1 cup short grain brown rice

1½ Tbsp. coconut oil

½ red onion, finely diced

½ red pepper, chopped

½ orange pepper, chopped

2 cloves of garlic, minced

1 tomato, diced

4 pork sausages, sliced in rounds

2 cups chicken broth

1 tsp. thyme

1 tsp. cayenne pepper

1 tsp. crushed bay leaf

½ tsp. paprika

½ tsp. sea salt

¼ tsp. parsley, chopped

4 cups water, divided

pepper

KUNG PAO CASHEW CHICKEN

SERVES: 4 | TOTAL TIME: 40 MINUTES

Kung Pao Chicken, or Gōngbǎo jīdīng as it's known in China, has an origin story is of hope! In the early 19th century, a boy named Ding Baozhen was saved from drowning by a man. When he grew up, he decided to visit his hero's home—where he was served the first Kung Pao Chicken. He was surprised and became its' biggest fan. He asked the family for the recipe and continued to make it for himself and others. It gained popularity and became a very popular dish for tourists and in American-Chinese cooking as well.

DIRECTIONS

1 Whisk together 3 tablespoons of soy sauce, 4 tablespoons of flour, oyster sauce, half the coconut oil, ginger and garlic until a runny paste forms. Marinate cubed chicken for 30 minutes.

2 Whisk together the remaining soy sauce and flour, as well as the vinegar, brown sugar, water, and tomato paste and set aside in a small bowl. Heat remainder of coconut oil in a wok. Add in red peppers and sauté for 3-5 minutes until browned. Add in cashews and sauté along with peppers for another minute. Transfer to serving bowl.

3 Add in pieces of chicken to hot wok and cook until the chicken's coating has evenly browned, about 6-7 minutes. Add in peppers and cashews and sauté for another few minutes. Pour in the sauce and stir to evenly coat chicken and peppers in the sauce.

Serve hot Kung Pao chicken on top of jasmine rice or basmati rice, garnished with sesame seeds and green onions.

INGREDIENTS

7 Tbsp. soy sauce, divided

6 heaping Tbsp. of all purpose flour, divided

2 Tbsp. oyster sauce

1½ Tbsp. coconut oil

1 clove of garlic, minced

4 chicken breasts, cubed

2 tsp. brown sugar

¼ cup white vinegar

2 Tbsp. water

½ Tbsp. tomato paste

½ tsp. fresh ginger, grated

1 small red pepper, chopped

½ cup of cashews

sesame seeds, to garnish

chopped green onions, to garnish

Raw Virgin
Huile de noix de

MOO GOO GAI PAN

SERVES: 4 | TOTAL TIME: 35 MINUTES

Moo Goo Gai Pan is traditionally a Chinese-Cantonese feature in home kitchens; however, the way we eat it now in restaurants has become somewhat Americanized (much like other Chinese food favorites). Because of the simplicity of the ingredients and taste, it is thought that Moo Goo Gai Pan comes from modest origins. "Moo Goo" in Cantonese means "mushrooms", and Gai Pan means "Sliced Chicken." This dish has popularized the stir frying of meat and vegetables together!

INGREDIENTS

- 1½ Tbsp. soy sauce
- 1 tsp. white vinegar
- 1 tsp. cornstarch
- 2 large chicken breasts, sliced into thin pieces
- ½ Tbsp. coconut oil, melted
- 4 cloves garlic, minced
- 3 cups white mushrooms, sliced in half
- 2 cups sugar snap peas
- 1 can sliced bamboo shoots, drained
- 1 can sliced water chestnuts, drained
- 1 tsp. cayenne pepper

FOR THE SAUCE

- ½ cup chicken broth
- 1 Tbsp. soy sauce
- 1 Tbsp. white vinegar
- ½ tsp. honey
- ½ tsp. coconut oil

DIRECTIONS

1 In a large bowl, whisk together (for the marinade, not the sauce) the soy sauce, white vinegar, and cornstarch. Add in sliced chicken breast and toss to coat with the mixture. Set aside for 30 minutes.

2 While the chicken is marinating, Heat the coconut oil in a wok. Brown the garlic, and toss in the mushrooms. Sauté for 3-4 minutes until the mushrooms have softened. Add in snap peas, bamboo shoots, water chestnuts, and cayenne pepper. Sauté for another 2-3 minutes.

3 Whisk the ingredients for the sauce in a small bowl, and set aside. Transfer the cooked vegetables to a separate plate and allow to cool. Drop the marinated pieces of chicken in the wok where you cooked the vegetables (there should be enough oil from the cooked vegetables to cook the chicken through). Cook the chicken over medium heat until the coating has evenly browned, about 6-7 minutes.

4 Add in the vegetables and toss everything together for 1-2 minutes before drizzling the sauce into the wok. Once the sauce is in the wok, lower the heat and stir to evenly coat chicken and vegetables. Sauce will thicken after 4-5 minutes.

Serve your moo goo gai pan on its own for a filling lunch or with cooked brown rice.

BLOOD ORANGE MOROCCAN TAGINE CHICKEN

SERVES: 6 | TOTAL TIME: 45 MINUTES

Tagine is a Moroccan delicacy that is enjoyed by people all over Africa and all over the world. The dish gets its name from the vessel traditionally used to cook it; the tagine. The tagine is a clay pot with a cone for a top that is used to cook meats like chicken and lamb. The clay pots are unglazed and bring out the natural flavor and color in the ingredients that they hold. It was first introduced to Moroccan culinary arts in the 12th century by the Phoenicians. Some food historians maintain that it appeared as early as the 9th century, based on the stories of *The Thousand and One Arabian Nights*.

DIRECTIONS

1. In a large skillet, heat coconut oil. Add in onions and sauté until translucent. Add in ginger and sauté for 1 minute. Add in chicken pieces and cook until there is no pink showing. Add in cayenne pepper, sea salt, allspice, turmeric powder, honey, and blood orange juice. Bring to a simmer.
2. Add in blood orange pieces and cilantro and stir to combine. Cook for another 5 minutes over low heat. All the liquid should evaporate.

Serve your Moroccan tagine chicken garnished with pistachios and fresh cilantro.

INGREDIENTS

2 lbs. chicken breasts, cut into bite sized pieces

½ Spanish onions, diced

1-inch piece of fresh ginger, grated

1 tsp. cayenne pepper

1 tsp. sea salt

½ tsp. allspice

½ tsp. turmeric powder

juice of ½ a blood orange

¼ cup of blood oranges, chopped

1 tsp. honey

2 Tbsp. coconut oil

¼ cup cilantro, chopped

handful of pistachios, to garnish

PANANG CURRY CHICKEN AND NOODLE BOWL

SERVES: 2 | TOTAL TIME: 20 MINUTES

We can all thank Thailand for Panang curry—an aromatic blend of spices that are typical to Thai cooking. Thai cooking has been influenced by its neighbors, but is very unique in its use of certain flavors. In Panang curry, kaffir lime leaves are a huge part of the taste and smell. While there are many famous curries originating from Thailand (Red, Masaman, Yellow), Panang curry is the perfect balance for those who don't like too much spice, but love the flavors of cilantro, cumin, and chilies.

DIRECTIONS

1 In a small, powerful blender, blend together all the ingredients for the curry paste until completely smooth and runny.

2 In a wok, heat coconut oil. Add in onions and ginger. Sauté until onions become translucent. Add in vegetables and sauté for another 3-4 minutes. Add in chicken pieces and cook until no longer pink. This will take about 6-7 minutes. Transfer the curry paste into the wok and mix the cooked chicken and vegetables with the paste thoroughly.

3 Add in coconut milk and chicken broth. Simmer for 10 minutes. Add in honey, chili pepper flakes, and hoisin sauce and stir for 2-3 minutes. About ¼ of the liquid should evaporate. Add in the cooked noodles and toss to coat in the soup. Squeeze the lime into the soup and stir for a few minutes.

Serve your Panang Curry Noodle Bowl hot, garnished with cilantro and crushed peanuts.

INGREDIENTS

FOR THE CURRY PASTE

½ cup red chilies
¼ cup red onion, diced
3 cloves garlic
1 stalk of lemongrass
1-inch of fresh ginger, peeled
2 Kaffir lime leaves or 2 tsp. lime juice
¼ cup water (or more)
½ Tbsp. crunchy peanut butter
¼ tsp. cumin
1 Tbsp. cilantro, chopped

FOR THE CHICKEN AND NOODLE BOWL

½ Tbsp. coconut oil
½ red onion, minced
1 Tbsp. fresh ginger, grated
2 cups matchstick carrots
2 cups red peppers
1 large chicken breast, thinly sliced
1 cup coconut milk
½ cup chicken broth
1 Tbsp. honey
1 Tbsp. chili pepper flakes
2 tsp. hoisin sauce
½ a fistful of flat rice noodles, cooked
juice of half a lime

QUICHE LORRAINE

SERVES: 5 | TOTAL TIME: 1 HOUR

Surprisingly, quiche was not a French creation. In fact, it originated in Germany where is was called "kuchen," or "cake." The original quiche was an open pie with a filling of egg, creamy custard, and bits of bacon–much like the quiche we eat today at brunches. The addition of cheese and onions came later. After the end of the second world war, quiche became increasingly popular in Europe; especially in England, but considered to be a woman's meal because it didn't contain any meat!

DIRECTIONS

1. Preheat oven to 350 degrees. Grease a 9-inch pie dish with coconut oil. Unroll pie crust and press into the pie dish. Use a fork to docket the base. Freeze for 20 minutes. Line a baking sheet with parchment paper and lay out 6 bacon strips and bake in the oven for 15 minutes. Flip each strip with a spatula and cook for another 10-15 minutes or until browned and crispy. Transfer bacon to a paper towel lined plate. When cooled, crumble into bits.
2. While bacon is cooking, heat coconut oil in a small skillet. Sauté onions with the brown sugar. Sauté until onions are translucent and slightly browned. Set onions aside off the heat.
3. Bake the pie crust for 20 minutes in the preheated oven. Meanwhile, in a large bowl, whisk whole eggs, pepper, salt, and nutmeg, together for 2-3 minutes until frothy. Whisk egg whites separately until white and foamy yielding soft peaks. Pour egg whites into the egg mixture, and whisk for another minute. Pour in milk and whisk again.
4. Remove pie crust and let cool for a few minutes. Increase oven temperature to 400 degrees. Add onions, cheese, chives, and crumbled bacon to the base. Pour the egg mixture over the base of the pie crust.
5. Bake quiche for 10 minutes in 400 degrees, then reduce the temperature to 375 degrees and bake for another 40 minutes until the eggs have set, and the crust has browned.

Serve each quiche in slices for brunch!

INGREDIENTS

- 12-inch pie crust (store-bought or homemade)
- 6 strips of smoked bacon
- 1 tsp. coconut oil, plus extra for greasing
- ½ Spanish onion, finely sliced
- ½ tsp. brown sugar
- 3 whole eggs
- ½ tsp. sea salt
- ½ tsp. ground pepper
- ¼ tsp. ground nutmeg
- 3 egg whites
- 1½ cup non-fat milk
- ½ cup of low fat, shredded cheese
- 2 tablespoons chives, finely chopped

SHEPHERD'S PIE

SERVES: 5 | TOTAL TIME: 1 HOUR

Shepherd's pie, sometimes referred to as cottage pie, is a British staple comfort food: meat and potatoes! Traditionally, shepherd's pie is made with ground lamb, not beef. Cottage pie was the name for the beef comfort food that we know today, however, the name of Shepherd's Pie caught on. There have been several versions of Shepherd's Pie throughout the years, but the exact origin is shrouded in mystery. Some British cookbooks in the 1920s have mentions of a dish similar to Shepherd's pie. A popular author, Lloyd-Hughes, notes that there were similar stews and dishes emerging from Ireland and Scotland around the same time.

DIRECTIONS

1 Over medium heat, boil potatoes in chicken broth and water. Cook until potatoes fall off a fork. Drain the chicken broth into a large bowl and remove potatoes from the heat. Mash the potatoes, adding in ¼ of the chicken broth back into the potato mash. Add in sour cream, salt and pepper. Mash until potatoes are creamy and without lumps. Set mashed potatoes aside.

2 In a saute pan, heat coconut oil. Saute onions and diced vegetables for 1-2 minutes until the onions are translucent. Add in ground beef, another ¼ cup of the reserved chicken broth, chili powder, and Worchester sauce and cook over low heat until beef has cooked through.

3 Preheat oven to 375 degrees. Layer the beef and vegetables on the bottom of an ovenproof pan. Spoon and spread mashed potatoes on top of the beef layer. Use a fork to make a design on the mashed potatoes, and garnish with chives.

4 Bake in the preheated oven for 30-40 minutes, until the potatoes just start to brown.

Serve a slice of shepherd's pie sprinkled with shredded cheese.

INGREDIENTS

3 large russet potatoes, peeled and quartered

2 cups of chicken broth

1 cup of water

¼ cup light sour cream

1 tsp. ground pepper

½ tsp. sea salt

2 Tbsp. coconut oil

1 yellow onion, diced

1½ cup mixed vegetables (carrots, peas, corn), diced

1 pound ground beef

5 Tbsp. Worchester sauce

1 tsp. chili powder

chives, to garnish

SAUCY SLOPPY JOES

SERVES: 6 | TOTAL TIME: 40 MINUTES

Sloppy Joes are meaty, saucy, and so very filling. Most people source this culinary delight to Sioux-Falls, Iowa in the 1930s. A talented cook named Joe added tomato sauce to his already delicious loose meat sandwiches. An instant star was born, and the creation became a popular order throughout restaurants in the States.

DIRECTIONS

1 In a large skillet or wok, heat coconut oil and sauté garlic and onion until garlic is browned and onions are translucent. Add in celery, orange pepper, carrots, and sauté for 2 minutes. Add in beef and cook until it has browned and cooked through. Drain the fat and place on low heat.

2 Add in remaining ingredients and simmer for 8–10 minutes, stirring to combine well.

Serve your Sloppy Joes on Kaiser rolls or ciabatta buns with a side of pickles.

INGREDIENTS

1 Tbsp. coconut oil

5 cloves of garlic, minced

½ a Spanish onion

2 stalks of celery, diced

1 orange pepper, diced

¼ cup of matchstick carrots, finely chopped

1 lb. extra lean ground beef

1 cup tomato sauce

¾ cup tomato paste

2 Tbsp. Worchestershire sauce

½ Tbsp. chili pepper flakes

½ tsp. cayenne pepper

6 Kaiser rolls

GRILLED CHICKEN SOUVLAKI SKEWERS

SERVES: 2 | TOTAL TIME: 15 MINUTES

Souvlaki dates back to Ancient Greece, where it was traditionally made with lamb. Now, however, chicken souvlaki has become popular all over the world; and believe it or not, recognized as Greek "fast food" despite being so healthful. In its original form, souvlaki was cooked over an open flame over hardwood charcoal. This charbroiling technique of cooking meat is typical to Mediterranean tastes.

DIRECTIONS

1 In a bowl, mix together coconut oil, yogurt, garlic, lemon juice and zest, oregano, Himalayan salt, cayenne pepper, ground coriander. Mix in chicken pieces and coat in the marinade. Marinate for at least 30 minutes or up to a day.

2 Heat your grill pan and brush coconut oil on liberally. Skewer the pieces of chicken (5-6 pieces of chicken per skewer) and grill on medium high heat on one side for 4 minutes and then grill on opposite side for 3-4 minutes until chicken is cooked through.

Serve your Chicken Souvlaki within a pita drizzled with tzatziki.

INGREDIENTS

2 Tbsp. coconut oil plus extra for grill pan

1 heaping Tbsp. fat-free yogurt

3 cloves garlic, minced

juice of ½ a lemon, plus zest

½ tsp. oregano

¼ tsp. pink Himalayan salt

¼ tsp. cayenne pepper

¼ tsp. ground coriander

2 chicken breasts, cut into bite sized pieces

SPAGHETTI BOLOGNESE

SERVES: 8 | TOTAL TIME: 1 HOUR

Bolognese sauce is one of the only pasta sauces that originally didn't contain a heavy base of tomato. Although most people do add tomato to Bolognese sauce nowadays, it's mostly there for color and to act as a binding agent. True to its name, Bolognese sauce originates from Bologna, Italy, although some food historians have noted that it may have originated in Imola, a town just west of Bologna. Historically, Bolognese sauce was made primarily with red wine and minced beef and small amounts of cream, tomatoes and butter. Now, for affordability, vegetables, and milk are added in larger amounts.

DIRECTIONS

1. In a large pot, heat the coconut oil. Sauté the onion, carrots, celery, and garlic. Sprinkle in the salt and sauté until the onions are translucent. Add in the meat and mix thoroughly, breaking the meat up into little pieces as it browns.

2. Pour in the milk. Add the chopped oregano, and cover the pot and cook over medium heat for about 20 minutes. The milk should boil. Stir intermittently.

3. Add in the beef broth, diced tomatoes, tomato sauce, basil, and nutmeg. Stir while the mixture comes back to a boil. Sauce should be thick and meaty. Add in the parmesan and stir until the cheese melts into the sauce.

Serve your Bolognese sauce over cooked spaghetti, garnished with basil.

INGREDIENTS

½ Tbsp. coconut oil

1 yellow onion, minced

3 carrots, peeled and finely diced

4 stalks celery, diced

6 cloves garlic, minced

1 tsp. sea salt

1 lb. ground chuck

1½ cups milk

1 tsp. fresh oregano, chopped

2 cups beef broth

2 cups diced tomatoes

1 cup tomato sauce

5 leaves of basil, chopped

pinch of nutmeg

¼ cup parmesan cheese, grated

8 cups cooked spaghetti

UNDER THE SEA

BAJA FISH TACOS

SERVES: 3 | TOTAL TIME: 1 HOUR

Also known as Tacos de pescado, most people agree that fish tacos were first created in Ensenada–a port town in the Mexican state of Baja California. Mexico, a country renowned for its colorful and flavorful culinary art, was a fitting birthplace for the dish. The modern fish taco originated in the 1950s, and became increasingly popular in the American diet.

DIRECTIONS

1. In a medium sized bowl, whisk together coconut oil, cilantro, cayenne pepper, cumin, lime juice, smoked paprika, chili pepper flakes, and salt. Line a baking sheet with parchment paper and preheat your oven to 375 degrees.
2. Pour the marinade in a shallow dish and put the haddock filets in the shallow dish and use your hands to massage the marinade onto the filets. Place each filet onto the baking sheet. Bake for 10 minutes in the preheated oven. Use a spatula to flip each filet oven and bake for another 15 minutes. Remove from pan and chop.
3. Whisk together the Greek yogurt and pepper in a bowl. Assemble each taco by layering equal red cabbage, chopped fish, then a drizzle of Greek yogurt mixture on a tortilla.

Serve your baja fish tacos garnished with fresh cilantro.

INGREDIENTS

1 lb. boneless, skinless haddock filets (3 filets)

½ Tbsp. coconut oil, melted

1 Tbsp. cilantro, chopped

1 tsp. cayenne pepper

½ tsp. cumin

juice of one lime

¼ tsp. smoked paprika

½ tsp. chili pepper flakes

½ tsp. salt

3 Tbsp. Greek yogurt

½ tsp. pepper

½ cup red cabbage, chopped

3 tortillas

CRISPY CRAB CAKES

SERVES: 5 | TOTAL TIME: 20 MINUTES

Crab cakes; flaky on the inside, and crispy on the outside. They're a restaurant favorite, and Marylanders are proud to claim responsibility for the original composition of the crab cake. The crab cakes we know now are quite recent, popping up only in the 20th century, but the process of using seafood and bread together and turning it into a croquette has been a time honored tradition—partially because seafood was popular, but also because mixing in bread and other ingredients was cheaper than using 100% seafood in the patties.

DIRECTIONS

1. Brush a skillet liberally with coconut oil and heat over low heat.
2. Drain the crabmeat and transfer to a large bowl and mash/shred with a fork. Add in red onion and cilantro and mix to evenly disperse. Whisk in eggs one at a time.
3. Add in remainder of ingredients except for panko and mix thoroughly. Add in panko at the very end and mix again. Form a patty with your palms and shallow fry two at a time for 4-5 minutes on the first side.
4. Flip each patty when the sides look browned (about 4-5 minutes). Cook for another 4-5 minutes after flipping.

Serve hot with a garlic aioli sauce.

INGREDIENTS

coconut oil for shallow frying

2 tins of chunks of crabmeat

½ red onion, diced

¼ cup cilantro, chopped

2 eggs

1-inch of fresh ginger, grated

juice of 1 small lime

zest of ½ a lime

3 tsp. fat free plain Greek yogurt

½ tsp. chili powder

¼ tsp. salt

½ cup panko (bread crumbs)

BATTERED FISH AND OVEN CHIPS

SERVES: 4 | TOTAL TIME: 1 HOUR AND 30 MINUTES

Churchill loved fish and chips. he called them "good companions." There are multiple origin stories; but it's agreed that this power couple exploded in the late 1800s in the United Kingdom. After European migrants sensed the impending success of fish and chips, shops all over the UK began popping up and giving the people what they wanted: a crispy and delicious comfort food!

DIRECTIONS

1 Heat oven to 425 degrees and line a baking sheet with parchment paper. Soak the thick slices of potato in a bowl of ice cold water for 15-20 minutes. Drain and dry. In the same bowl, toss together coconut oil, chives, salt, pepper, oregano, cayenne pepper, and paprika with the potatoes. Bake in the oven for 15 minutes, then flip oven chips with a spatula and bake for an additional 15 minutes. Reduce the temperature to 350 degrees, flip again and return to the oven for an additional 10 minutes.

2 In a shallow, large bowl, sift together flour, cornstarch, baking powder, garlic, salt, and pepper. Add in chicken broth slowly and use a rubber spatula to combine. Be sure not to over mix. The batter will be viscous and lumpy. Add in lemon juice and mix again. Batter will become smoother.

3 Heat 1½ tsp. of coconut oil in a skillet. Turn the heat to medium high. Rub the fish filets with plain flour on each side and dip into batter until completely coated in thick batter. Once oil has heated, carefully lower your coated filet into the pan with a spatula. Pan will sizzle. The batter will start to bubble on top. Cook on first side for 3 minutes and then flip filet over and cook for an additional 2-3 minutes.

4 Transfer finished filet to a paper towel lined plate and let the excess oil be soaked up. Repeat for each filet.

Serve your fish and chips immediately with a side of tartar sauce and ketchup.

INGREDIENTS

FOR THE OVEN CHIPS

3 baking potatoes, sliced into ½-inch thick strips

1 Tbsp. coconut oil

1 Tbsp. fresh chives, chopped

1¼ tsp. salt

1 tsp. ground pepper

1 tsp. oregano

½ tsp. cayenne pepper

⅛ tsp. paprika

FOR THE BATTERED COD FILLETS

1 cup flour plus extra for rubbing filets

¼ cup cornstarch

1 tsp. baking powder

½ tsp. garlic powder

½ tsp. salt

¼ tsp. pepper

1¼ cup of chicken broth

juice of 1 lemon

(6 tsp.) 1½ tsp. coconut oil per filet

4 frozen cod filets (100 grams each), defrosted

NASI GORENG

SERVES: 4 | TOTAL TIME: 40 MINUTES

Nasi Goreng, literally translated, means "fried rice" in Malay. This traditional Indonesian rice dish combines shrimp, rice, eggs, and a whole lot of flavor. The stir fry process was adopted by Indonesians and Malaysians from Chinese influence. The influence probably originated in the 12th-15th centuries when trade between China and Indonesia was at their height.

INGREDIENTS

1 Tbsp. coconut oil, melted

4 shallots, finely diced

2 cloves garlic, minced

¼ tsp. salt

1 tsp. oyster sauce

3 red chilies, chopped finely

1 Tbsp. honey

1 tsp. tamarind

1 Tbsp. tomato paste

2 Tbsp. kecap manis (sweet soy sauce)

3 cups basmati rice, cooked

10 cooked shrimp

5 green onions, chopped

2 eggs

DIRECTIONS

1 In a large wok, heat the coconut oil. Add in the shallots and garlic. Sauté until shallots have browned. Add in salt, oyster sauce, chilies, honey, tamarind, tomato paste, and sweet soy sauce. Mix with a spatula and add in the cooked rice. Stir to coat the rice in all the spices and sauces.

2 Toss in the shrimp and green onions and stir into the rice. Create a little well in the rice and crack an egg in the well. Use a fork to scramble the egg. Disperse the egg throughout the rice once cooked.

3 In a separate pan, cook the last egg sunny side up.

Serve your nasi goreng with a fried egg on top, and fresh green onion pieces to garnish.

SUMMER SHRIMP ROLLS

SERVES: 5 | TOTAL TIME: 20 MINUTES

Specific to Vietnamese cuisine, fresh spring rolls like these are healthier than the deep fried rolls that most restaurants serve. The ingredients are fresh and flavorful. In Vietnamese, these fresh rolls are called "Goi Cuon" meaning "salad roll" and they are emblematic of Vietnamese cuisine. The fillings change from kitchen to kitchen, but traditionally, pork and shrimp are the main fillings for Goi Cuon.

DIRECTIONS

1 In a small saucepan, heat the coconut oil and sauté shrimp for 1 minute on each side. Add in ginger, cayenne pepper, and salt and toss for 1 more minute.

2 Set shrimp aside in a bowl. Clean your counter and set up a large, shallow bowl filled with water. Submerge two sheets of rice paper together until soft. Lay your rice paper on the work surface. First roll vermicelli and ⅕ of the carrots inside a lettuce leaf and place in the middle. Lay out three shrimp above the roll of lettuce, and one basil leaf in between each shrimp. Roll like a spring roll, tightly. Repeat for remaining 4 rolls.

Serve your shrimp rolls cold with a spicy peanut dipping sauce.

INGREDIENTS

½ tsp. of coconut oil

15 cooked shrimp, defrosted

1 tsp. ginger, grated

pinch of cayenne pepper

pinch of salt

10 sheets of rice paper

½ cup of vermicelli, toasted in coconut oil

1 cup of matchstick carrots

5 leaves of lettuce

10 basil leaves

SNACKS AND SIDES

ALOO TIKKI

SERVES: 6 | TOTAL TIME: 1 HOUR

Aloo Tikki is a North Indian croquette made with potatoes, onions (usually), cilantro, and a blend of aromatic spices that is traditionally served with mint chutney, tamarind sauce, and yogurt. Aloo is literally translated as "potato" and Tikki means "cutlet" in Hindi, Mahrati, and Tamil. Aloo Tikki is served in cafés (called Dhabas) and street food carts all over India, Bangladesh, Pakistan, and Nepal as a popular vegetarian snack; often served between slices of bread.

DIRECTIONS

1. In a medium sized pot, boil vegetable broth over medium-high heat. While the broth is heating, peel the potatoes and chop into quarters for a faster boiling time. Once vegetable broth is boiling, drop the potato pieces into the pot carefully and cover.
2. While potatoes are boiling, mix together bread crumbs, mint, cornstarch, cilantro, cumin powder, and garam masala in a small bowl.
3. Test your potatoes by inserting a fork into a piece. When the potato slides off the fork on its own, the potatoes are done (about 15 minutes). Drain the broth and set the potatoes aside to cool slightly. As soon as they are cool enough to handle with bare hands, grate the potatoes finely or mash with a fork. 5 medium-small potatoes should yield approximately 3 cups of boiled, grated potato.
4. In a large bowl, add grated potatoes, chilies, ginger, lemon juice, and your mint/cilantro/spice mix. Mix with a rubber spatula just until combined. Add salt and pepper to taste.
5. Heat coconut oil in a frying pan. Ensure that the entire pan has a thin layer of heated coconut oil before proceeding (you can do so by brushing the pan with a pastry brush that has been dipped in the coconut oil). Form a 3-inch patty shape with the potato mixture and shallow fry in the heated coconut oil for 2–3 minutes on each side until both sides are evenly browned and crispy.

Serve your aloo tikki hot with a side of chutney, and garnished with fresh cilantro.

INGREDIENTS

- 2 cups vegetable broth
- 5 medium-small yellow or white potatoes
- ¼ cup unseasoned bread crumbs
- 2 Tbsp. fresh mint leaves, finely chopped
- ½ Tbsp. corn starch
- ¼ cup cilantro leaves and stems, finely chopped
- ½ tsp. cumin powder
- ½ tsp. garam masala
- 4 red chilies, chopped
- 1 tsp. fresh ginger, grated
- juice of ½ a lemon
- salt and pepper to taste
- ½ Tbsp. coconut oil

CARAMELIZED ONION AND BACON GALETTE

MAKES: 3-5 GALETTES | TOTAL TIME: 40 MINUTES

Traditionally, galettes were served in bakeries all across France with a sweet pastry filling or candied fruit and called "galette des rois"–or King Cake. However, there have been many savory variations on galettes that serve as great appetizers at parties and weddings. The tradition of King Cake dates back to Roman times, when a bean was hidden in one of the hundreds of galettes served. The one who found the bean was celebrated as a king for a day, as the bean was tied to superstitions of fertility.

DIRECTIONS

1. Preheat your oven to 400 degrees and line a baking tray with parchment paper. Heat the coconut oil on medium-high in a skillet and add in the diced red onion. Sauté for about a minute, until onion turns translucent. Add in brown sugar to caramelize. Sauté until the onions have browned, about 5 minutes. Take the skillet off of the heat and toss the onions with thyme. Transfer to a separate bowl.
2. Cook the bacon on the hot pan until browned. Chop into tiny pieces. Cut puff pastry into 8-inch circles with a cookie cutter or any circular object. Scallop the edge by cutting little triangles around the edge. Layer 2 tablespoons of feta cheese in the center of the puff pastry, 2 tablespoons of caramelized onions, and top with 2 tablespoons of bacon and ½ a tablespoon of feta cheese. Top with thyme leaves. Fold the scalloped edges over each other to seal in the filling. Do the same for each remaining galette.
3. Whisk together the egg and water and use a pastry brush to brush over each galette liberally.
4. Transfer each galette to the baking tray lined with parchment paper. Bake for 15 minutes in the preheated oven.

Serve each galette hot from the oven (reheat in the oven on low heat).

INGREDIENTS

- 1 Tbsp. of coconut oil
- 1 red onion, diced
- ½ tsp. of brown sugar
- ½ tsp. of white vinegar
- 2 sprigs of Jamaican or regular thyme, stripped (plus extra to garnish)
- 5 strips of bacon (turkey bacon works as well)
- ½ cup light feta cheese
- 2 sheets of puff pastry, thawed and unrolled
- 1 large egg
- 1 tsp. water

PAN-FRIED GYOZA

SERVES: 4 | TOTAL TIME: 45 MINUTES

More commonly referred to as dumplings or pot stickers, the first versions of Gyoza originated in China where it is still known as jiaozi; however, it is most commonly associated with Japanese cuisine. Gyoza was introduced to Japan in the 1940s, during World War II—after Japan invaded China in the 1930s. This event in history is said to have prompted soldiers to bring home Chinese dumpling-making techniques to Japanese kitchens.

DIRECTIONS

1 Heat 1 tablespoon of coconut in a frying pan. Add ginger, chili flakes, and garlic powder to the heated oil and mix until ginger starts to brown. Add green onions and soy sauce and cook for 30 seconds before adding vinegar and ketchup.

2 Add ground meat to frying pan and cook through until meat is coated in the marinade and is no longer pink, about 5 minutes. Use cooking utensil to crumble meat into smaller pieces. Drain fat and set meat aside on a plate lined with a paper towel to soak up excess fat/oil.

3 Keep your open dumpling wrappers covered with a damp paper towel to keep them from drying out or cracking. Place a small amount of cooked meat into the center of a round dumpling wrapper and wet the edges. Fold wrapper in half, sealing the meat in. Repeat until all the meat is used.

4 In the same frying pan used to cook the meat, heat the remaining ½ tablespoon of coconut and lightly fry the dumplings on one side until it is golden-brown and crispy.

Serve your pan fried gyoza hot with any spicy sauce, and garnished with scallions and sesame seeds.

INGREDIENTS

1½ Tbsp. coconut oil, divided

2 tsp. fresh ginger, grated

1 tsp. chili pepper flakes

½ garlic powder

¼ cup green onions, chopped (plus extra to garnish)

2 Tbsp. soy sauce (plus extra for serving)

1 Tbsp. white vinegar

½ Tbsp. ketchup

1 lb. ground pork or ground chicken

1 package round wonton/gyoza wrappers

sesame seeds, to garnish

SPICY POTATO LATKES

SERVES: 8 | TOTAL TIME: 45 MINUTES

Potato latkes are a thin and crispy pancake made with battered potatoes. Originating in Poland, Latkes are linked to Jewish cooking. In the 1800s, the Jewish community was fondly regarded as the culinary masters of the potato. The earliest latkes were a combination of cheese, grated potatoes, and onions. Now, recipes include varied spices and ingredients. The first Latke recipe was brought to USA at the end of the nineteenth century as a part of one of the first Jewish-American cookbooks, *"Aunt Babette's Cookbook: Foreign and Domestic Recipes for the Household."*

DIRECTIONS

1. Soak the julienned potatoes in a bowl filled with ice water. Soak until ice melts completely. Drain water and air dry.
2. Return potatoes to large bowl and pour in beaten eggs, flour, bread crumbs, spices, and lemon juice. Mix all the ingredients together with a rubber spatula until all potato pieces are covered in the "batter."
3. Heat a third of the coconut oil in a skillet and add a ½ cup of the potato mixture and flatten into a pancake shape. Add two more ½ cups of potato mixture and fry 3 latkes without crowding. Fry on one side for 3-4 minutes until it can be easily flipped and is golden brown. Cook on the second side for 2-3 minutes. Transfer to a paper towel lined plate and cook remaining potatoes the same way.

Serve the latkes hot topped with sour cream and chopped cilantro or chives.

INGREDIENTS

6 medium potatoes, sliced julienne

2 eggs, beaten

¼ cup all purpose flour

⅛ cup bread crumbs

1 Tbsp. chili pepper flakes

1 tsp. garlic powder

1 tsp. ground pepper

½ tsp. onion powder

juice of ½ a lemon

4 Tbsp. coconut oil

SNACKS AND SIDES

JOLLOF RICE

SERVES: 8 | TOTAL TIME: 45 MINUTES

Jollof rice is a hugely popular side dish in Western Africa. A point of contention between Ghanians and Nigerians, this unique dish has caused quite an uproar over its origin. The name for jollof rice comes from the Wolof people in Africa. The earliest origin can be traced to the Senegambian region, ruled by the Jolof Empire. Some food historians believe that the spread of Jollof rice in Africa came hand in hand with the Mali Empire.

DIRECTIONS

1 In a pan, heat coconut oil over medium-high heat. Add onions to the pan and cook until translucent. Add in garlic, ginger, chilies, salt, paprika, and cumin. Mix well.

2 Pour in rice and toast for 3-4 minutes. Add in vegetable broth, crushed tomatoes, and thyme leaves. Stir until all the ingredients are combined. Cover the pan and simmer for 15-20 minutes. Stir intermittently until all the liquid has evaporated.

Serve jollof rice garnished with fresh cilantro and as a side to a meat curry or with fried plantain.

INGREDIENTS

½ tablespoon coconut oil

¼ a Spanish onion, diced

2 cloves of garlic, minced

1 teaspoon of crushed ginger

3 red chilies, chopped

½ teaspoon salt

½ teaspoon paprika

¼ teaspoon ground cumin

2 sprigs of thyme, de-stemmed

½ cup of basmati rice, uncooked and washed

1 cup of vegetable broth

¾ cup crushed tomatoes

cilantro, to garnish

PIEROGIES

SERVES: 6 | TOTAL TIME: 40 MINUTES

A favorite Polish appetizer, pierogies have transcended the borders of Poland and become a crowd pleaser all over Europe and North America. Pierogies have been a staple in Polska cuisine since the 13th century, and are made during celebrations and holidays. These dumplings first appeared in Polish cookbooks in the 17th century. Although other countries have laid claim to the invention of pierogies, they are widely regarded as a jewel of Polish culinary history.

DIRECTIONS

FOR THE DOUGH

1. In a large bowl, sift together the flour and salt. Make a little well in the center of the flour and pour in warm milk, water, and coconut oil. Use a spatula to mix the ingredients together. Once the dough comes together, turn it out onto a floured surface and knead for a few minutes until the dough is smooth. Let the dough rest for 10 minutes while preparing the filling.
2. In a small skillet, heat ¼ tsp. of coconut oil and sauté the shallots and garlic until garlic has browned.
3. Fill a pot with water and bring to a boil. Boil the potatoes until they fall off the fork. Drain the water and mash the potatoes. Add in shredded cheese, cooked shallots and garlic, salt, pepper, cayenne pepper, and sour cream. Mash again until potatoes are completely smooth.
4. Roll the dough out on a floured surface. Cut dough into 5-inch circles. Add a tablespoon of the filling in the center of each circle of dough. Wet the edges of the dough and seal by pressing the dough together. Brush each pierogi with remainder of the coconut oil and place on a heated skillet or on a baking sheet. If baking, bake for 8–10 minutes. If using a skillet, heat up the pierogis for 1-2 minutes on each side until browned.

Serve your pierogis with sour cream, garnished with chives and bits of bacon.

INGREDIENTS

FOR THE DOUGH

- 3 cups all purpose flour
- pinch of salt
- ½ cup warm milk
- ½ cup water
- 1 Tbsp. coconut oil, melted

FOR THE FILLING

- ½ tsp. coconut oil
- 4 shallots, diced
- 2 cloves of garlic, minced
- 3 large russet potatoes, peeled and quartered
- ¼ cup shredded mozzarella
- salt and pepper, to taste
- ½ tsp. cayenne pepper
- 2 Tbsp. sour cream

BAKED POUTINE

SERVES: 4 | TOTAL TIME: 1 HOUR

This quintessentially French-Canadian dish is a combination of cheese, gravy, and French fries. Although many restaurants claim the right to the invention of poutine, there is one widely known story that begins in Warwick, Quebec in a restaurant named Le Lutin qui Rit. A customer requested gravy and cheese curds on his fries, to which the owner responded, "Ça va faire une maudite poutine," that when translated, means: "That's going to make a dreadful mess."

DIRECTIONS

1 Line a baking sheet with parchment paper and preheat your oven to 400 degrees. Submerge sliced potatoes in ice water and let sit for 15 minutes and then drain. Let the potatoes dry on paper towel.

2 In a bowl, mix sliced potatoes with 1½ teaspoons of melted coconut oil, oregano, paprika, salt, and ½ teaspoon ground pepper. Line unbaked fries on parchment paper without overlapping. You may need more than one batch. Bake in preheated oven for 40 minutes, using a spatula to flip fries over at 15 minute intervals. Increase oven temperature to 425 degrees and bake for an additional 5 minutes.

3 While the fries are baking, prepare the gravy by melting the remaining coconut oil over medium high heat. Add in all purpose flour and stir until a paste has formed. Add in chicken broth, garlic powder, and remainder of pepper. Stir until mixture has thickened. If mixture is too thin, add more flour.

4 Once fries are done, top with gravy and cheese curds.

Serve your poutine hot in a shallow bowl. Place some cheese curds on top of hot fries and pour gravy on top so the cheese curds melt. Top off with extra cheese curds and fresh parsley.

INGREDIENTS

- 2 large baking potatoes, sliced julienne
- 1 Tbsp. + 1½ tsp. coconut oil, divided
- 1 tsp. oregano
- ½ tsp. paprika
- ½ tsp. salt
- 1½ tsp. ground pepper, divided
- ¼ cup all purpose flour
- ¾ cup chicken broth
- ¼ tsp. garlic powder
- ½ cup white cheddar cheese curds

ROASTED RED PEPPER AND BASIL HUMMUS

SERVES: 6 | TOTAL TIME: 20 MINUTES

Hummus has a somewhat ambiguous beginning. We can all agree that wherever it came from, it is a powerhouse of flavor! An abundance of chickpeas in the Middle East made the creamy dip inexpensive. The word "hummus" literally means "chickpeas" in Arabic. Middle Eastern countries have fought over the origin of hummus for ages and no conclusion has been reached, but each country puts their own flair into hummus–how much tahini is used, how much cumin or garlic, or the oil they use in the preparation.

INGREDIENTS

½ a red pepper, sliced

2½ cups chickpeas, drained and rinsed

3½ cloves of garlic

juice of ½ a lemon

¼ cup water

4 Tbsp. tahini

2 Tbsp. coconut oil

1 tsp. salt

1 tsp. ground pepper

½ tsp. cumin seeds

½ tsp. chili powder

½ tsp. smoked paprika

2 fresh basil leaves

DIRECTIONS

1. On a hot pan over medium heat, roast red pepper slices until they have started to blacken. Cool before handling.
2. Add all ingredients to a food processor and pulse until completely smooth and creamy.

Serve crispy pita brushed with coconut oil with your hummus and top with chopped red peppers and basil.

CLASSIC GUACAMOLE

SERVES: 6 | TOTAL TIME: 25 MINUTES

Believe it or not, the Aztec civilization came up with guacamole in the 1500s, calling it "ahuaca-mulli", which translated, means "avocado sauce." The recipe was undoubtedly passed down from generation to generation, and today, guacamole is probably one of the most popular Mexican dips for tortilla chips! The Aztecs were big believers in consuming avocados daily since they believed them to be aphrodisiacs. Avocados are extremely healthy, containing loads of healthy fats and plant protein.

DIRECTIONS

1. Preheat your oven to 200 degrees and line a baking sheet with aluminum foil. Brush tomatoes, red onion, and garlic with coconut oil. Wrap in aluminum foil and place in the oven for 10 minutes.
2. While the oven is on, de-pit the avocados and scoop them out of the peel and mash with a fork in a large bowl. Add in lime juice, cilantro, sea salt, cumin, cayenne pepper, and ground pepper. Remove the tomatoes, garlic, and onion from the oven and let cool.
3. De-seed the tomato and dice finely. Mince the roasted garlic and the red onion. Add to the bowl of seasoned, mashed avocados and mix thoroughly.

Serve your guacamole with tortilla chips or on a slice of whole wheat toast

INGREDIENTS

1½ tomatoes

1 small red onion

2 whole cloves of garlic

½ tsp. coconut oil, melted

5 ripe avocados

juice of half a lime

3 Tbsp. cilantro, chopped

1 tsp. sea salt

½ tsp. cumin

½ tsp. cayenne pepper

½ tsp. ground pepper

ROMANIAN CHIFTELE

SERVES: 8 | TOTAL TIME: 55 MINUTES

Chiftele, much like kofta in Mediterranean cooking, is a meatball or mini flat patty of a mixture of meats, herbs, spices, and breadcrumbs. Variants of chiftele are eaten all over the Balkans as well as in Northern African countries. Chiftele's flavors and preparation have traces of Turkish culinary traditions–no coincidence, considering that the Ottoman empire occupied Romania for centuries.

DIRECTIONS

1 Line a baking sheet with parchment paper and preheat your oven to 425 degrees.

2 Heat ½ a teaspoon of coconut oil in a skillet and sauté the garlic and shallots until shallots have browned, about 5 minutes. Grate the potatoes into the skillet and cook until potatoes are tender-about 15 minutes. Remove from heat and let the onion/potato mixture cool.

3 In a large bowl, use a rubber spatula to mix together pork, beef, eggs, panko, cilantro, dill, Worchestershire sauce, salt, and pepper. Add in the grated potatoes-onion mixture. Using your hands, roll a heaping tablespoon of the mixture with your hands. Place onto the prepared baking sheet. Repeat until you have 24 meatballs. Bake in the preheated oven for 30-35 minutes, until browned.

Serve your chiftele on mini buns or with a toothpick as an appetizer with a dipping sauce.

INGREDIENTS

1 tsp. coconut oil

6 shallots, finely chopped

3 cloves garlic. minced

2 potatoes, peeled

1 lb ground pork

½ ib ground beef

2 eggs

½ cup Panko

¼ cup cilantro, finely chopped

2 Tbsp. dill, finely chopped

1 tsp. Worchestersire sauce

salt and pepper to taste

SPICY PLANTAIN CHIPS

SERVES: 2 | TOTAL TIME: 30 MINUTES

Plantain and Banana chips are popular in various tropical regions of the world. In Indonesia, banana chips called kripik pisang are popular. Spiced plantain chips are especially popular in Guyana, Ghana, and in many South and Central American countries like Peru and Ecuador. They are traditionally fried in coconut oil, but can also be baked. Plantains are eaten this way wherever they grow—Latin America has used plantains in a myriad of ways in street food and more sophisticated dishes. The history of plantain dates back to Malaysia in 500 B.C. In 327 B.C., when, Alexander the Great, in his travels, came into contact with the fruit, the fruit was introduced to Europe and Africa. Today, African countries still use plantain heavily in their cooking. In a different part of the world, plantain was made popular in the 1500s, after a Portuguese monk stumbled upon the fruit in the Canary Islands.

DIRECTIONS

1. Grease a large baking sheet with half the coconut oil. Preheat the oven to 350 degrees.
2. Cut the ends off the plantain and score the peel deeply. Peel the plantain and slice it into thin rounds (about ¼-inch thick). Toss the rounds with the remainder of the coconut oil, cayenne pepper, and sea salt.
3. Lay the plantain rounds in one layer on the greased baking sheet (do not layer rounds on top of each other or the chips will not crisp up like chips). Bake for 30 minutes. Use a spatula to move chips around after 20 minutes to ensure that they aren't sticking to the sheet.
4. Transfer hot chips to a paper towel lined plate and wait until they cool.

Serve your chips on their own, or on the side of rice and chicken!

INGREDIENTS

1 large plantain

½ Tbsp. coconut oil

½ tsp. cayenne pepper

½ tsp. sea salt (or more)

SWEET POTATO GRATIN

SERVES: 2 | TOTAL TIME: 1 HOUR AND 10 MINUTES

Gratin is often referred to as Gratin Dauphinois because of its origin in the Dauphine region of France. It is generally baked in a shallow dish with scalloped potatoes mixed with cheese and cream. In 17th century France, however, cheese was not included in gratin because it was too expensive.

DIRECTIONS

1 Using a mandolin cutter or a sharp knife, slice two sweet potatoes to 1/16th of an inch. Submerge slices in ice water. Preheat your oven to 400 degrees and grease a small 8×8 casserole dish or a small cast iron skillet with coconut oil.

2 After 15 minutes, drain the ice water and add garlic, coconut oil, nuts, parsley, honey, paprika, pepper, and ground coriander.

3 Arrange the slices of sweet potato in concentric, overlapping circles in the pan. Cover with aluminum foil and bake in preheated oven for 30 minutes. Bake uncovered for another 25 minutes.

Serve your gratin as a side dish to poultry or in a wrap.

INGREDIENTS

2 medium sweet potatoes

1 clove of garlic, minced

1½ Tbsp. coconut oil, plus extra for greasing

¼ cup chopped walnuts or pecans, toasted

½ tsp. parsley

½ tsp. honey

½ tsp. paprika

¼ tsp. ground pepper

⅛ tsp. ground coriander

TURKEY PELMENI

SERVES: 6 | TOTAL TIME: 35 MINUTES

These famous dumplings are the pride of the Russians. Filled with spiced meat, these dumplings are almost tortellini-esque in shape, but completely different in taste. Pelmeni is similar to another Eastern European dumpling called Vareniki which is similar to pierogis. Pelmeni is accepted to have been a product created in the Ural mountains by Russian pioneers. It was derived from pelnyan, or "ear-bread" that consisted of meat wrapped in very thin bread dough, much like modern pelmeni.

DIRECTIONS

1 In a skillet, heat coconut oil and sauté shallots and garlic until garlic has browned. Add in ground turkey, lemon juice, chili flakes, salt, and pepper. Break the turkey up into little pieces and cook until turkey has browned. Drain the fat and set aside.

2 Using a 4-inch circle cookie cutter, cut the dumpling wrappers into circles and place beside a shallow bowl of water. Add a tablespoon filling in the center of each circular wrapper and wet the edges of the dumpling wrapper. Fold in half and seal. Fold the two ends towards each other, mimicking a tortellini shape. Continue to make little dumplings until you use all the filling.

3 Boil a pot of water and drop in 5–8 dumplings. When dumplings float to the surface of the boiling water, use a slotted spoon to remove them from the water. Place on a serving plate. Boil all the dumplings this way. Once all of the dumplings have finished boiling, toss the dumplings in the vinegar. Garnish with chopped, fresh parsley.

Serve your pelmeni hot with any spicy dipping sauce.

INGREDIENTS

½ Tbsp. coconut oil

4 shallot, finely diced

2 cloves of garlic, minced

1 lb. ground turkey

2 Tbsp. lemon juice

1 Tbsp. chili pepper flakes

½ tsp. salt

½ tsp. pepper

1 package dumpling wrappers

3 Tbsp. white vinegar

parsley, finely chopped to garnish

KISIR/COUSCOUS SALAD

SERVES: 3 | TOTAL TIME: 30 MINUTES

Traditionally, kisir is a Turkish tomato and bulgur wheat salad; however, couscous is a similar alternative and an easier find in some areas. It yields the same kind of texture and taste as traditional kisir. There are multiple variations that include pomegranate seeds, cucumber, and lettuce, and different preparations are native to different areas of Turkey. The consensus is that kisir is meant to be eaten cold, the same way that a salad is.

DIRECTIONS

1. In a small saucepan, heat coconut oil and sauté shallots and garlic until garlic has browned and shallots are translucent. In a separate pot, heat the vegetable broth and bring to a boil. Add in couscous and stir intermittently until water starts to evaporate.

2. Lower the heat and add in cooked shallots and garlic, lemon juice, tomato paste, cilantro, chili flakes, pepper, and salt. Stir and cook until all the water has evaporated and the couscous is red.

Serve your kisir as a side to curries, poultry, or as a snack on its own!

INGREDIENTS

½ tsp. coconut oil

3 shallots, finely diced

1 clove garlic, minced

1 cup vegetable broth

¾ cup couscous, rinsed

juice of half a lemon

2 Tbsp. tomato paste

2 Tbsp. cilantro, chopped

½ Tbsp. chili pepper flakes

1 tsp. pepper

½ tsp. salt

INDEX

ABOUT THE AUTHOR

RITIKA GANN grew up happily eating and exploring. Her love for international cuisine stems from her adventures in Europe, North America, Asia, and South America. She is the creator-owner of the food blog *R&M Cooks*. *Coconut Oil: 65 Recipes for Cooking Clean* is her first cookbook, but she plans to keep writing, cooking, and learning about food. Ritika currently lives in Little Rock, Arkansas, with her husband.